THE FICTION OF REALITY

The Fiction of Reality marks a new direction in literary criticism. A writer, pondering the question of existence, finds his mind invaded by images from several novels; a memory of fictions becomes his immediate reality. Remembered fictions, as real as the butterflies in the writer's perception, appear as a vivid experience and become a more persuasive reality than the world of objects. The fictions of several writers (including Beckett, Virginia Woolf, Alain Robbe-Grillet, Patrick White and Machado de Assis) enter the writer's mind as realities to replace his own: they both intensify the torment of existence and alleviate it by gradually transforming the writer to *the other*. For finally, the writer's own reality is overwhelmed by the fictions his mind has been absorbed by, and the words he finds himself repeating as though they were his own are not his but of a character in a novel. The critic's reality becomes dissolved in a fiction, and the language created on the page to capture the experience within the critic's mind becomes a book called *The Fiction of Reality*.

Zulfikar Ghose (himself a widely admired novelist) has made of literary criticism a work of the imagination. Writing criticism in the tradition of W. H. Auden and Paul Valéry, he brings, with the force of an original mind, an illuminating understanding as well as an exquisite delight to the reading of fiction. Fully aware of the recent post-Structuralist trends in criticism, he scornfully ignores fashionable points of view to invent his own imaginative approach. The general reader will find this book refreshingly readable, its witty prose a source of considerable pleasure; the scholar will welcome it for its innovative approach and for its stunningly new perceptions into many important texts.

Zulfikar Ghose is Professor of English at the University of Texas at Austin. He was born in Pakistan in 1935, grew up in British India and came to England in 1952. Finishing his education at Keele University, he worked as a cricket and hockey correspondent of the *Observer* for five years. In 1969 he left England for the USA and since then has lived in Austin.

He has published nine novels, including the trilogy *The Incredible Brazilian*, a book of short stories (with B. S. Johnson), an autobiography, three volumes of poetry and a critical work, *Hamlet, Prufrock and Language*.

By the same author

CRITICISM
Hamlet, Prufrock and Language

POETRY
The Loss of India
Jets from Orange
The Violent West

AUTOBIOGRAPHY
Confessions of a Native-Alien

FICTION
Statement against Corpses (*stories, with B. S. Johnson*)
The Contradictions
The Murder of Aziz Khan
The Incredible Brazilian
   The Native
   The Beautiful Empire
   A Different World
Crump's Terms
Hulme's Investigations into the Bogart Script
A New History of Torments
Don Bueno

THE FICTION OF REALITY

ZULFIKAR GHOSE

First published 1983 by
THE MACMILLAN PRESS LTD
London and Basingstoke
Companies and representatives
throughout the world

ISBN 0 333 29093 3

Typeset in Great Britain by
WESSEX TYPESETTERS LTD
Frome, Somerset
Printed in Hong Kong

A hunter fires his gun in a forest, his victim falls, he rushes forward to seize it. His boot strikes an ant hill two feet high, destroys the ant house, and scatters ants and ant eggs all around. . . . The most philosophical of the ants will never be able to understand that black, enormous, terrifying body: the hunter's boot that burst into their house with unbelievable rapidity, preceded by a terrifying blast and a flare of reddish flame.

STENDHAL: Red and Black

The Fiction of Reality

Sometimes I think; and sometimes I **am.** (Valéry). One can be sitting beside the ligustrum bushes with their snow-white blossoms in early summer, the butterflies folding and unfolding their wings as they cling to the perfumed essence and the bees moaning in the delirium of the sweetness from the blossoms which seems to be over-whelming them as they attach themselves now to one and now to another powdery dot in the cluster of white blossoms surrounded by new glossy leaves; and one can be content with the purity of sensation, leaving the mind to flit unchecked from one thought to another while the body absorbs the idle passions of the fragrant afternoon. One can be subsumed by the light which filters through the green leaves in that contentment with life when memories dissolve and the body is felt to possess that substantiality in which vague, but rich, odours become a solid presence. There is a whirling of colours as if the currents of the perfumed air were each a strip of the blue sky or a red pomegranate flower torn from the branch by a sudden, maddening gust. One sips, like Emily Dickinson, the nectar never brewed, one becomes a debauchee of dew. It is the exhilaration of a subtle and negative sort of awareness: of non-being, or the death of the self, when life is experienced only as a breath of perfumed air. One does not need to sniff cocaine to have hallucinations of rainbows and to see the swift flight of the hummingbird as a stillness of luminous green wings. In the dissolution of memories, in the novel belief that the self is momentarily freed from the afflictions of knowledge, becoming, during the brief experiencing of that ecstasy, the Other, one is filled then by an enchanting sense of a different being, and, in that giddy moment of beautiful confusions when one is dispossessed of the self, one asserts **I am.** No thought of contradiction attends such a bold affirmation. *And I begin again to ask myself what it could have been, this unremembered state which brought with it no logical proof of its existence, but only the sense that it was a happy, that it was a real state in whose presence other states of consciousness melted and vanished.* (Proust). But logical coherence forces attention to itself; the earlier consciousness, with its perception of things immediately at hand, returns. The mind will not be succoured by images of the forest or be thrilled by evocations of the ocean breaking on a tropical beach without being satisfied about the meaning of things. *Man's world is the world of meaning. It tolerates ambiguity, contradiction, madness, or confusion, but not lack of meaning. The very silence is populated by signs.* (Octavio Paz). The mind has a quarrel with reality, having for generations rejected definitions of it while seeking, with the craving of an addict, one more new interpretation. It will take up this thing or that, even the body of which it is both the sitting tenant and the rent collector, and be filled with despair at the incomprehensibility of existence. *I think; here I lie under a haystack. . . . The tiny space I occupy is so infinitely small in comparison with the rest of space, in which I am not, and which has nothing to do with me; and the period of time in which it is my lot to live is so petty beside the eternity in which I have not been, and shall not be. . . . And in this atom, this mathematical point, the blood circulates, the brain works and wants something. . . . Isn't it hideous? Isn't it petty?* (Turgenev). These whirling clusters of words, these images which enter the mind and become fragmented—the butterflies folding and unfolding their wings—all from fictions, and the black beady eye of the bee, for a fraction of a second the only visible phenomenon in my universe, receding at great velocity like a planet in space—but it has only moved to a farther branch. Groups of words, related to no immediate sensation, enlightening no personal experience, come and go like fireflies which create an extraordinary brightness for a moment and then leave the night darker. Amazing, the language that constructs itself, then disintegrates, and again assembles in a slightly altered formation, as if the words were recalcitrant soldiers brought to group themselves in a column and could not be restrained from filling the air with a bawdy song. Do the peasants, working the fields within sight of Uxmal or Palenque, understand any less, or more, of the Mayans than the archaeologists from Europe or North America whose convictions carry a scientific aura? The arbitrariness of meaning, the foolishness of ideas! *The blind cells of hearing, in their obscure consciousness, must of necessity be unaware of the existence of the visible world, and if you were to speak to them of it, they would doubtless consider it an arbitrary creation of the deaf cells of sight, while the latter in their turn would consider the audible world created by the hearing cells a complete illusion.* (Unamuno). When no group of words releases that meaning which would bring the solace of understanding, one then concludes that there is Nothing, for one will not be content with intermediate states, with provisional truths, just as a child who has been denied the orange it has demanded then refuses to eat any other fruit. Each thought that presents itself to the mind, coming with a brilliant promise, seems surrounded by a ring of bright moons of conviction, but when its course is exhausted the darkness of Nothing becomes even more intense. *The mysteries of a universe made of drops of fire and clods of mud do not concern us in the least. The fate of a humanity condemned ultimately to perish from cold is not worth troubling about. If you take it to heart it becomes an unendurable tragedy.* (Conrad). Such nihilism, too, is unbearable, and one finds it the most objectionable when it appears to be the most convincing. The idea of existence can appear so appalling that it can be accepted only by those with a strong religious faith, who must find a Conrad or a Beckett an 'inhuman thinker'. *If consciousness is no more—as some inhuman thinker said—than a flash of lightning between two eternities of darkness, then there is nothing more execrable than existence.* (Unamuno). And, in a milder language, Tolstoy: *And if you really think that death is after all the end of everything, then there's nothing worse than life either.* But for Conrad, *Faith is a myth and beliefs shift like mists on the shore; thoughts vanish; words, once pronounced, die;.* Of the many uses of words the most obsessive one concerns the invention of reality which must daily be shaped somehow not only in our normal dealings with our families and colleagues at work to whom we must make the effort not to appear to be lunatics but also in the abstract world of our own inner silence which has to be filled with those words which soothe, clarify, bring meaning. But we've been made fools by the language we've invented by imposing upon it the burden of meaning and by charging it that it contain a capacity for truth. But it is only *as though one were anxious about the cut of one's clothes in a community of blind men. . . . Half the words we use have no meaning whatever and of the other half each man understands each word after the fashion of his own folly and conceit.* (Conrad). The compulsion to invent a believable reality remains strong, however; hence, the enormous universal consumption of fiction. One would think that an age so conscious of the pressures of time would have no time for novels; far from it: more novels (to say nothing of the fictions available on television) are consumed now than ever before, and what is more, some of the popular novels that become world-wide best-sellers are longer than *War and Peace*! Look about you the next time you are in a packed jumbo jet; even when a movie is on there will be several people reading a fat paperback. It is not simply the inane desire to escape from oneself but a craving, perhaps, to see the world created anew: we lend credence to one more fiction to see if it will not create that impression of reality which will convince us of its truth. *And so it goes on, from story to story, from fiction to fiction in an unceasing endeavour to express something of the essence of life.* (Conrad). Even when it comes to abhor the notion of existence, the meaninglessness of which so appals it, for it has seen Nothing, the mind will not cease from inventing another, and then another, language to see whether a significant vision has not eluded it; it will continue to create fictions although it has concluded that all former combinations of signs and symbols have explained nothing. As in Beckett—*my life a voice without quaqua on all sides words scraps then nothing then again more words more scraps the same ill-spoken ill-heard then nothing vast stretch of time then in me in the vault bone-white if there were a light bits and scraps ten seconds fifteen seconds ill-heard ill-murmured ill-heard ill-recorded my whole life a gibberish garbled six-fold*—the mutterings of an existence which will never lose a knowledge of its own being while never gaining knowledge of anything else. In Beckett's fictions, the human body is first grotesque, then crippled and finally only an idea in the mind of the speaker as we follow the existence of Murphy and Watt, Molloy, Malone and the Unnamable. But the mind remains a ceaseless babbler, recalling images of a dead past which it does not always believe in and giving a farcical and an obscene utterance to philosophical thought. In Dostoevsky's St Petersburg and Patrick White's Australia, the hero finds himself in a desert where he must confront the failure of the body which he has himself unconsciously tried to annihilate. But Raskolnikov's quest for salvation drowns in the sentimentality of a contrived ending after much rain has indeed fallen over St Petersburg, and Voss, whose realistically described journey across the desert is a solemn and rather portentous version of Molloy's comical progress through the bog and the heather, must die without seeing his vision: the city streets will again be parched and dusty, the desert will remain a vast, meaningless tract of sand. The possessed mind, like Voss's, is perhaps only suffering from an organic disorder: a brain fever. In Conrad's Far East or in his Africa, the mind searches for a bearable reality or an explanation of it. There is none. Virginia Woolf's characters have intimations of words which just fail to come to their lips. There is the anguish of time passing; and however brilliant the sunset, it is merely the end of another day that brought no knowledge; some whisper a formula of prayers, hoping for the body's continued health and expressing pious attachments to family, country and God, while others, whose despair with existence has long abandoned such convictions, mutter with Beckett's character: *and all this business of above yes light yes skies yes a little blue yes a little white yes the earth turning yes bright and less bright yes little scenes yes all balls yes the women yes the dog yes the prayers yes the homes yes all balls yes*—for the world of the family, the dog and the communal faith is not the point: it might be solid enough, and real too, but what is this other world in which I exist? The universe, which has its modern fictions in the writings of Einstein and Heisenberg, could well be a dream in the mind of a frail, blind old writer, Borges. And space as described by the novelist could belong to a physicist's perception—as in Beckett: *Molloy, your region is vast, you have never left it and never shall. And wheresoever you wander, within its distant limits, things will always be the same, precisely. . . . But now I do not wander any more, anywhere any more, and indeed I scarcely stir at all, and yet nothing is changed.* Or Conrad's *vast and uncertain expanse, as of a crepuscular horizon on a plain at dawn—or was it, perchance at the coming of the night?* One can go back to Balzac and find in him the Beckettian perception: *Man is a clown walking the tight-rope over the void.* One can be confined in a nutshell, like Hamlet, and be king of infinite space, but one's condition is scarcely different from Molloy's lying helplessly in bed. Nothing is changed, except this changing body—*this cataclysm of being* (Paz)—with its loquacious mind endlessly pursuing abstractions to allay the anguish of existence. Reality remains a presumption, a story of the world that is now convincing and now filled with the confusions of a dream imagery, and every attempt to be clear to oneself about the nature of reality ends in the elaboration of another fiction. The earth is flat and is the centre of the universe. The earth is a sphere in some undetermined spot in a universe. The earth is a speck of mucus escaped from the nose of a god who has sneezed. We inhabit one world, or another. Or another. *Life is full of alternatives but no choice*, says Patrick White. The alternatives are fascinating because they are all fictions, each one carrying the potential of that surprise which will be the meaning we need. They are stories in which we want to know what's going to happen next and in which we long for a surprise ending while remaining in terror of the nature of the surprise; or the fictions are an absence of stories made up of a deliberately ungrammatical utterance, an anti-language, to see what revelation might be had by distortion; or they are the dreams of a mind which has never asserted—because no one has ever asked it—that it has ever been awake. Borges suggests it in his *Ficciones*: all systems of knowledge are a fiction; or that each fiction is a system of knowledge. Philosophy is a fantastic form of literature and literature a fantastic form of philosophy. We live out myths and myths are created by our lives; we remember stories and we are the characters in the stories that others tell. Even one's own life with its accumulation of memories—those unscrupulous advocates of the self—becomes a fiction: Borges is obliged to live with 'Borges' and when writing a piece entitled 'Borges and Myself' must necessarily end with the words, *Which of us is writing this page I don't know*. And Unamuno, who found the concept of existence unthinkable without a faith which offered a life everlasting, could not help concluding: *The most liberating effect of art is that it makes one doubt of one's own existence*. The words come and go; the butterflies fold and unfold their wings. Entire fictions

spring up their images, and the mind staring emptily at
the white flowers on the ligustrum bushes and conscious
that the sky has suddenly darkened in the west and that
there will soon be a burst of rain, finds itself staring now at
a farm in Russia where Levin is mowing the grass and now
at Crusoe on his island in the mouth of the Orinoco.
Words come. *And words vanish, and nothing remains, do you*
understand? Absolutely nothing, oh foolish man! Nothing. A
moment, a wink of the eye and nothing remains—only a drop of
mud, cold mud, dead mud launched in black space, turning around
an extinguished sun. Nothing. Neither thought nor sound nor soul.
Nothing. Conrad's words, written in a letter in 1898,
remind one of Beckett's in *How It Is*, first published in
1961, where too there is mud and black space and Nothing
and where, as here, *alone in the mud yes the dark yes sure yes*
panting yes someone hears me no one hears me . . . with the rain
nearer now . . . the self sinking in the darkness. *And when*
my own face reappears, there is nobody there. I too have left myself.
(Paz). And entered . . . *the long course of my waking dream.*
(Proust).

Early in the history of the English novel, as one sees it with
Daniel Defoe, the novelist creates a fiction about himself
pretending that he is not inventing a reality but merely
editing the recorded facts of a true reality. 'The editor
believes the thing to be a just history of fact; neither is
there any appearance of fiction in it,' says Defoe in his
Preface to *Robinson Crusoe*. It is an attempt to eliminate the
idea of appearances and thereby to create a greater
conviction with which to anticipate the reader's possible
disbelief in the events to come: in announcing that he is
rejecting 'fiction' for 'a just history of fact' while *knowing*
full well that he is doing no such thing, the novelist is
informing the reader that fact itself cannot be trusted to
contain truth, especially as the novelist knows that the
reader has seen him wink and has not at all been taken in

by his declaration of being a mere historian. Fiction is not being identified as fact; fact is being proclaimed a fiction. The twentieth-century novelist—following Flaubert's dictum 'No lyricism, no comments, the author's personality absent'—denies himself the role even of an editor, preferring to give his fiction the same objective reality which any other fact of the universe might be deemed to possess. The novelist has become a medium through whom a text comes into existence and he will be the last person to assert that the *text* is anything but groups of sentences generating a meaning which is engendered only by the premises contained within the text, and it will be of no consequence to him if someone were to label the work *a novel*. While in Defoe the assumption is that the images being recorded—Crusoe's impressions of Africa (where tigers are to be seen!), for example—are a true and accurate record of what his hero has witnessed of the world, the twentieth-century writer who actually travels and sees the world creates fictions which have no relationship to what he has witnessed, for his fictions are constructs entirely of his imagination—as with Raymond Roussell who travelled around the world and although he wrote a novel entitled *Impressions of Africa*, declared in an autobiographical statement that 'from all these travels I never took anything for my books.' (Of course, there are modern novelists, like Hemingway and Graham Greene, who travel in search of subject matter or for an exotic setting but they are the makers of consumer products and are of no enduring value to the history of the human imagination).

But even in Defoe the objective reality presumed to be true is only an invention: Crusoe's island exists only in Defoe's mind and not in the mouth of the Orinoco. A writer needs to fulfil the pattern suggested by his imagination and not to complete a record of his character's existence. To all intents and purposes, *Robinson Crusoe* ends when Crusoe leaves the island; the happy ending in sight, the passage back to England does not need to be described, and Defoe does not do so; the words 'after a long voyage, I arrived in England' are enough. But the novel does not end there. Defoe obliges Crusoe to go to Lisbon on business and then invents a new situation for him to suffer; he takes Crusoe on a *land* journey from Lisbon for no other reason than an artistic one. Taking Crusoe and his party to the Pyrenees in winter, he puts them in a landscape of snow which is a representation, on solid ground, of the idea of the ocean, and there he surrounds them with hundreds of ravenous wolves whose 'growling kind of noise' and howling and yelling are not too subtle a representation of a howling gale upon the ocean. Indeed, when Crusoe, seeing 'some large timber trees, which had been cut down the summer before', draws his 'little troop in among those trees', the image is that of men crouching in a boat. Waves of wolves attack them and as water breaks over the bulwarks, so some of the wolves dash up over the barrier. The wolves 'came on like devils, those behind pushing on those before.'

The story does not need this additional example of the ordeals human beings have to suffer, but the writer's imagination is compelled to elaborate a metaphor in which the imagery is carefully ordered to hint that the previously described hazards on the ocean have also been a metaphor, thus transforming the history into a fiction. Truth is to be perceived not by looking at the world but by looking at the way in which images have been structured to complete the internal, imaginative order of the work.

Sometimes the images vividly present in our mind are not the representations of a world being perceived but are only a recurring event in the mind, being provoked by some association, which must play out a complete body of imagery which has accumulated from past perceptions and from past fantasies; an entire narrative plays itself out in a moment, the successive images not always being related causally. A man closing a door sees human figures in the grain of the wood and in the moment it takes him to complete the action of closing the door his imagination constructs the lives of the human figures, placing them in a city, giving them actions to perform and observing that those actions contain gestures and deeds which are an unconscious manifestation of deep-rooted racial memories. Thus a novel called *Project for a Revolution in New York* by Alain Robbe-Grillet gets written. 'I am closing the door behind me, a heavy wooden door . . .' he writes on the first page, '. . . in which I have discerned human figures for a long time'. And 181 pages later, in the last paragraph of the novel, he writes, '. . . and now I am closing the door behind me'.

The images which take several hours to read, and which to some readers are bewilderingly confusing, happen in the mind of the narrator in a passing moment. Reality is suggested by the habit of the mind to transform what one sees to that which it is not; we do not perceive a world of objects so clearly as the fictions generated in our minds by the same objects.

Cf. Valéry: 'We have the means of grasping what does not exist and of not seeing what hits us in the eye.' Valéry also wrote: 'All that our eyes really see is a question of chance.'

The 'revolution' in Robbe-Grillet's novel does not concern itself with political ideology. At first glance, the title *Project for a Revolution in New York* strikes one as a hoax, as if it had been calculated to catch the attention of a larger American audience than the author had previously enjoyed. Though apparently misleading, the title, however, is precise: the novel is a *project* and if the audience (and the publishers in New York!) were to understand it there would indeed be a revolution in New York, that city which has become the dictator of what cultural products the world may consume. For Robbe-Grillet, as well as every living novelist who cherishes his art, knows that the publishing industry in western Europe (and also in South

America, the new big market for consumer goods) has become a sycophantic slave of the New York publishers and that what New York most prizes is an abomination to a writer who takes the life of letters seriously; if only the *project* were to succeed, the New York publishers would at last be enlightened and would know what novels to promote: Robbe-Grillet's and anyone else's who produced a *new* novel! And the project could succeed if only the subtle design of *Project for a Revolution in New York* could be understood!

The first paragraph of the novel:

The first scene goes very fast. Evidently it has already been rehearsed several times: everyone knows his part by heart. Words and gestures follow each other in a relaxed, continuous manner, the links as imperceptible as the necessary elements of some properly lubricated machinery.

Scene, actors, words, gestures, imperceptible links. As in so much of Robbe-Grillet's work, one is again being reminded of a cinematic technique; but the paragraph itself is the first scene of a novel and is a statement of how first scenes of novels do get written. The author is not telling a story; he is creating a novel and in the process is obliged to show how the novel creates itself in the mind of the novelist. Suddenly something is there; not very clear in its outline at first: people, words, gestures, all yet to be defined; an intimation of images in the novelist's mind. This is followed by a pause when the novelist is groping to see what must come next. Thus, Robbe-Grillet's second paragraph:

Then there is a gap, a blank space, a pause of indeterminate length during which nothing happens, not even the anticipation of what will come next.

And that is precisely the novelist's situation: an image has come from nowhere, compelling the novelist to record it, and then left him wondering what should come next. It is not reality that he has to create, but those other images, those groups of sentences, which would most appropriately follow the first, given image. He is being driven less by what he knows of the real world and his own experience in it and more by what he knows of other fictions, including the ones he himself might already have created: their formal procedures, their style. It is after the pause suggested by the second paragraph that the writer withdraws, replacing himself with a narrator, an *I*:

And suddenly the action resumes, without warning, and the same scene occurs again . . . But which scene? I am closing the door behind me, a heavy wooden door with a tiny narrow oblong window near the top.

The opening of the novel, then, is a search for a point of departure which will take the novelist to a larger discovery—a discovery of those words with their clusters of images whose source is in memory, words which are needed to complete that form (*form*, not action) which, at the outset, is only a vague shape, and which, too, needs to be discovered by pausing again and again to see what should come next. Cf. Paz: 'Content stems from form, and not vice versa. Every form produces its own idea, its own vision of the world. Form has meaning; and, what is more, in the realm of art only form possesses meaning.'

And what comes next in *Project for a Revolution in New York* is a mosaic of images, a collage of visual impressions. Since written sentences can only work in a succession of horizontal lines while what is seen or experienced or contained by a consciousness at any given moment is a multiplicity of thoughts, images and sensations, therefore a narrative is obliged to produce a highly edited version of reality. The modern novelist has broken down that limitation by creating an artful confusion on the page; images are repeated with slight variations, what begins by appearing to be a description of a person ends up by being a poster in the subway, a tribal ritual turns out to be a documentary film on television. It might appear a frivolous enterprise unless the reader comprehends that the fragments of the mosaic, being elements of a perception and the data of sense impressions, reveal the experience of a particular consciousness, and that the general form of the confusion in the narrative is a truer expression of that experience than could be suggested by a clearly written traditional story. We are no longer looking at Julien Sorel or Emma Bovary or even Leopold Bloom; we are looking at *a novel*. The reader is not examining the states of mind of characters but is obliged to enter the consciousness of the writer himself, and that not in order to engage in some such portentous activity as understanding the human condition or the plight of the coal miners in Poland or West Virginia but to engage in an abstract perception of reality. Twentieth century painting has progressed towards the elimination of subject matter, and novelists have attempted a similar rejection of solid themes. And just as I, the reader, enter the consciousness of Robbe-Grillet, the novelist, similarly the critic, another *I* whose consciousness contains many previously assimilated texts, fragmentary images from several of which simultaneously come to mind in a moment together with some irrepressible bit of memory or personal association and the distractions present in the immediate field of perception, the critic, too, expresses his ideas in the form of a revelation of the imagery in *his* consciousness.

There is a description in *Project for a Revolution in New York* of an underground area devoted to amusements:

> slot machines whose enigmatic apertures, which respectively devour and spit forth change, are embellished so as to make more obvious their resemblance to

the female organ, games of chance allowing the player to lose in ten seconds some hundreds of thousands of imaginary dollars, automatic distributors of educational photographs showing scenes of war or copulation, pinball machines whose scoreboards include a series of villas and limousines, in which fires break out as a result of the movements made by the steel balls.

Reality has become a fantasy, money and country houses are make-believe possessions. The paragraph which follows describes souvenir shops where may be seen

arranged in parallel rows of identical objects, plastic reproductions of world capitals and famous structures, ranging, from top to bottom of the display, from the Statue of Liberty, the Chicago stock-yards, to the giant Buddha of Kamakura, the Blue Villa in Hong Kong, the lighthouse at Alexandria, Christopher Columbus' egg, the Venus of Milo, Greuze's *Broken Pitcher*, the Eye of God carved in marble, Niagara Falls with its wreaths of mist made out of iridescent nylon.

Buildings, gods, nature, works of art are reduced to plastic reproductions; all reality and interpretations of it (civilization, political declarations, religious beliefs, history, the works of artists) have become familiar clichés whose commonness diminishes that meaning which once expressed itself as fructifying emblems in a society. The reality of the past which shaped human kind has been reduced to plastic souvenirs which, stripping that reality of its original significance, render a distortion of it: the world is reduced to cheap replicas of its monuments, no one is actually looking at reality but at an invention of it.

In a passage which follows, the narrator finds himself in an underground cell where some fifty people who belong to some unspecified revolutionary cause are holding a meeting. Instead of relating the particular details of the meeting, the narrator uncovers the formal structure of the proceedings by making his observations as analytical generalisations:

> the meeting is given over to a kind of ideological discussion presented in the usual form, whose didactic effectiveness on the militants of every persuasion has been readily acknowledged: a prefabricated dialogue between or among three persons assigned alternately questions and answers, changing parts by a circular permutation at each shift of the text.

At one level, the writer seems to be presenting a social scientist's analysis of the rhetoric and symbols of a revolutionary movement; but at another level, that of the novelist uncovering the nature of reality, the writer is showing how human relationships occur as repetitions of formal patterns. There is a 'prefabricated dialogue' going on among the three persons, suggesting that however serious we believe our dialogue to be and however important we consider the ideas it contains, the dialogue inevitably follows the habits of a particular type of discourse. Everyone follows a text; and the phrase, 'each shift of the text', reminds the reader that he, too, has a text before him, a thought emphasised by the lines which follow in which Robbe-Grillet seems to hold up a mirror to his own novel:

> The sentences are short and simple—subject, verb, complement—with constant repetitions and antitheses, but the vocabulary includes quite a large number of technical terms belonging to various fields, philosophy, grammar, or geology, which keep turning up.

The fields of philosophy, grammar and geology are hardly the preoccupation of militants who meet in underground cells but they are certainly the preoccupation of a novelist

if 'geology' is understood as a metaphor for the world
inhabited by people. Thus a multiple ambiguity is
introduced in the passage before the reader: he is looking
at a meeting of militants, the formal structure of a
particular sort of human discourse, the constituents of a
novel, all at the same time while he is led to believe that he
is witnessing a startling reality. But a person reading a
novel is supposed to be reading *about* something; so,
Robbe-Grillet provides him with a subject:

> The theme of the day's lecture seems to be 'the colour
> red,' considered as a radical solution to the irreducible
> antagonism between black and white.

Human speech is sounds reflective of philosophical discourse (which discourse is only a recurring rhetorical
pattern with its own technical terms), and whatever
humanity does, its experience is reduced to symbols—a
procedure precisely that of the novel. The three persons
are referred to successively as speakers, actors and
performers, and just as their words have been prefabricated for them so have the actions, for they can do nothing
but repeat what has already happened. The novelist turns
anthropologist in one long sentence which includes references to 'religious rituals of Central Africa' and 'theatrical
performances of antiquity' to suggest the dynamic under-
lying the violence in New York, the sentence ending with
the brilliant perception, 'the staging of a mythology as
murderous as it is cathartic.' So, we are not seeing the
makings of a revolution in New York but are being given a
nearly Structuralist analysis of the city's violence and are
being shown that the prevalence of rape, arson and
murder is a function of the memory of the human race: a
mythologist, and not a social scientist, can reveal the
nature of the problem. A *revolution* has taken place in New
York in so far as some of the members of one of the most
advanced human tribes in the world is enacting in an

imagery which is modern the barbarous rites performed by their primitive forefathers; and the *project* is that which an anthropologist undertakes when he goes to study the rituals of a particular tribe.

The anthropological point is again taken up when a young woman is seen to be watching television while doing some ironing. What she is watching is 'a documentary film about the religious ceremonies of central Africa, in the course of which seven young girls of noble rank, belonging to vanquished tribes, are to be impaled on the sexual organ of the fertility god.' The film is entitled 'The Red and the Black', a not too subtle hint that what Stendhal's novel contains is not very different from the ceremonies of central Africa on the television screen since Stendhal too describes the rites of a society, and if one accepts that comparison then one is led to infer that the novel which is stating this parallel is itself describing a society. This suggestion is reinforced several pages later in a description of a playground where 'the black girls play like all children, performing what appear to be cruel and mysterious rites.' There are several other images scattered in the novel:

> they perform up and down the empty car an improvised dance on Sioux themes.

> they slowly perform around her a kind of wild dance, taking great silent steps, making broad gestures with their arms above their heads, sweeping and ceremonious salutations which, without any apparent or even symbolic meaning, seem nonetheless to belong to the ritual of some religious sacrifice.

> And now, for the last act, Joan's splendid bloodstained body is lying on its back, head down, on the altar steps of an abandoned church in the depths of Harlem which has been used for a long time for expiatory ceremonies.

The third quotation comes very near the end of the book and it is the only time that a 'ceremony' has been enacted in a place which is named, Harlem, and in a church which, however, is abandoned. If one remembers the earlier references to religious sacrifices and wild dances and re-examines the considerable body of imagery of violence of the primitive past and the technological present seen throughout the book, then one understands, just before the moment of closing the book, that the writer is completing a pattern and confirming a meaning. The Church has been abandoned; meaning has gone out of religious ritual; and yet the deep-buried instinct of the body to break out in a wild dance or to engage in sacrificial killing persists. Of course, we do not know what we do, for we have lost touch with the sources of our compulsive actions. This is not to say that there is a moral in the book, that we should again embrace the Church and all will be well. It is only to say that Robbe-Grillet, in showing all the barbarous sexuality and violence in his pages, is not at all being sensationalist; instead, he is being a very precise observer of society.

As he does in some of his other books, Robbe-Grillet includes ideas about the novel in *Project for a Revolution in New York*. The narrator picks up a book and leafs through it, 'pretending to be interested in the adventures of the characters.' (Robbe-Grillet, of course, has a contempt for characters, as we know from his essay 'On Several Obsolete Notions'; and incidentally, the word 'pretending' in that quotation introduces a nice joke to be appreciated by those who know Robbe-Grillet's opinions). But the book which the narrator has picked up turns out to contain the images of the novel in the reader's hands, and so it is part of the project in so far as it is concerned with the notion of creating a revolution about the idea of a novel. In this passage the narrator notices, 'in skimming the novel, that of the three elements of the secret in the heroine's keeping, one was known by the reader, the second by the narrator himself, and the third by the book's author alone.' The words ascribed to a narrator are invariably an insufficient representation of the author's ideas, and the reader, formulating his own interpretations, ascribes ideas to those words which the writer has not intended. The reality even of a fiction becomes an altered fiction in the reader's mind and he alone is the witness of the reality he has invented for himself.

In another passage, the narrator appears to be interrogated by a police officer whose questions concern the contradictions in the narrative. It is humorous to hear him say, 'your sentences are for the most part correctly constructed, though sometimes a little loose', but one notes in the narrator's 'confession' the statement 'you can't tell everything at the same time, so that there always comes a moment when a story breaks in half, turns back or jumps ahead, or begins splitting up'—and that, of course, is Robbe-Grillet's definition of his own method of creating fiction and also, as the dialogue, which proceeds for several pages, implies, a statement about the way reality operates. In one sense, the *project* has been to justify the forms of Robbe-Grillet's fictions.

Claude Simon's novel *Triptych* is made up of descriptive sentences and often a succeeding sentence has no connection with the one which it follows. It is a world of pictures and, indeed, the first set of sentences in the novel are pictures of a picture:

> The postcard shows an esplanade bordered by a row of palm trees standing out against a sky of too bright a blue, at the edge of a sea of too bright a blue. A long cliff of blinding white façades, with rococo decorations, follows the curve of the bay in a gently-sweeping arc. Exotic shrubbery and clusters of cannas are planted

between the palm trees, forming a bouquet in the foreground of the photograph.

At the end of the novel a man is completing a jigsaw puzzle and a few seconds after he has had the satisfaction of seeing the completed picture, 'his right hand violently sweeps back and forth across the surface of the table, breaking up the puzzle and scattering the little pieces all about.'

Some of the images seen on the jigsaw puzzle seem familiar and the reader has the impression that they come from the earlier parts of the novel, creating the conviction that he has only been watching the making of a picture which its maker could only glimpse in parts as he went about putting it together. There is no *meaning* at the end but one is left with a quantity of images in one's mind; and *that* is the meaning, one supposes: reality is a succession of sensations coming to us through the medium of descriptive sentences, a flowing procession of images some of which keep repeating themselves for no apparent reason and some which frustratingly interrupt others, distracting one from some thought to observe the features of a pleasing fantasy. The novel, then, is a precise statement of a consciousness and the experience it relates is the experience of being. To be is to have sensations invade the consciousness in no particular order.

The images in *Triptych* could comprise clear and complete events in themselves. There is a boy sitting at a desk, working on a problem in geometry; we see his calculations and his crossing out of the entire page; at one point he pulls out a drawer which contains a picture of a nude woman and proceeds to masturbate. But the prose—always objective, drawing no distinctions between a dead rabbit, a problem in geometry or the urge to masturbate since for the novelist all events in the world are merely phenomena to be described—does not invite the reader to interpret the event which he witnesses. In any case, even if the reader arrived at an interpretation and elaborated, say, a statement about the psychology of youth, nothing would have been proved.

There are several passages in *Triptych* which describe sexual activity between a man and a woman, some of them quite deliberately pornographic. But since we do not know who the protagonists are, our sympathy is not engaged; it is an event, during the occurrence of which, we are voyeurs, no different from the two boys holding up the strip of film against the light to see the action which we are seeing. The prose is flat and suggests no emotion, focusing on tiny details of the body:

> When the man lifts one of his hands up from the breast that it has been kneading, one can see the palm of it, of a lighter colour than the top, which has been tanned by the sun. The creases of the palm and the folds at the joints of the fingers form sharp black lines, like those in the hands of tractor drivers and mechanics, in which dirty oil and grease become encrusted in indelible streaks. . . . The skin is of a darker brown than the rough-surfaced nipples of the breasts that appear from time to time as the man's hands move back and forth.

The insistence is on what a thing looks like; the writer's fidelity is only to precision with which the thing is drawn; emotion and ideas are not his concern. Even those objects of the body which are most poignantly engaged in sexual activity and which in a novel of the traditional variety would be described in an effusive prose expressive of that poignancy are treated by Simon as if they were no different from any other set of objects:

> Shaped like short corrugated cylinders, the nipples jut out from the center of large swollen areolas, of a paler brown tinged with a bluish gray cast by the veins that flow through them and marble the white skin all around

them. Unlike the man's hands, the girl's hands, one of which is still tightly clasping the base of the erect penis, are light-coloured on the top, with the reddened skin of the palms furrowed by the sort of very fine little wrinkles, like countless tiny cuts, that tend to become more and more numerous through constant contact with wash-water and wet floor mops.

Of course, the references to mechanics, dirty oil, wash-water and floor mops is giving us information about the kind of couple we are looking at and the detailed dwelling on what the hands of each look like is serving the function of playing an amusing trick on the reader who, as any novelist well knows, is anxious to get to the really smutty part. And surely, 'short corrugated cylinders' has to be the absurdest simile ever invented to represent nipples. But the fact is that when we look at any phenomenon—a breast or a hand, say—we sometimes look at the entire object in its general form, sometimes at that aspect of it which makes it peculiarly itself, and sometimes at markings and disfigurations upon it which could well cover only a minute area of that object. But Simon's detailed imagery of the hands, affecting to be scientific in its observation, also serves the function of seeming to insist upon the reader that he, too, look at the images in the same objective way. So that when the writer comes to that element in the scene which may be considered porno-graphic—'one can finally see nothing except the glans across which the tip of the pink tongue is gliding back and forth'—the writing itself maintains its scientific cool as well as the pretence that accurate representation of a world of things is its sole concern.

A description of rabbits ends with these two sentences:

Their silky hairs become sparser inside their long ears, the pink skin of which is visible, and around their lips, which are also pink. Their muzzles quiver rapidly and continuously.

This is followed, without a break, with the sentence:

> Now and again the woman raises her head and her lips
> that have been pressed tightly around the cylindrical
> shaft of the member, and then around the glans, allow
> the latter to appear, swollen and hard, bright pink in
> colour, gleaming with saliva.

Another longer sentence continues and concludes the
pornographic picture. And then, again without a break,
there is this sentence of what the rabbits have been eating
and where they live:

> Little round bits of carrots, reddish-orange in colour
> with a pale green centre, along with other vegetable
> debris and dark brown pellets of dung, are strewn over
> the floor of the cell-like cages.

In the field of perception all phenomena are equal.
Rabbits in cages, a tongue gliding over a penis, vegetables
strewn in cages: the eye does not see a distinction between
them other than that suggested by colour and texture: the
rabbits' fur is gray, the glans of the man's penis is bright
pink, the carrots are reddish-orange and have a pale green
centre. The reference to colour in each of the three images
confers an equivalence upon them, the writer carefully
demonstrating by presenting three slides, as it were, that
each image carries the same amount of visible significance
and, therefore, none need be seen to possess a profounder
idea than the other two. Several events, each independent
of the other, take place simultaneously in the universe and
if we happen to observe two or three at the same time in
the duration of a few moments, it is a presumption to
conclude that they have a bearing on one another. That, of
course, was, and remains, the convention of the old-
fashioned novel; almost any sentence in *Middlemarch* can
be related to, and indeed depends upon, the rest of the

text. The world which generated the earliest English novels was created by Newton, given a philosophical justification by Locke and held together by the Protestant faith; all that collapsed with Heisenberg, Wittgenstein and the post-Darwinian bankruptcy of theology.

God is perhaps the man at the end of *Triptych* who has been amusing himself completing a jigsaw puzzle and, bored with what he sees when the picture is complete, wipes it off the table and lets the little pieces fall into the void.

And yet one can look at *Triptych* as a novel which in its outline resembles a work, say, by Stendhal. The opening description of the picture on the postcard with its 'long cliffs of blinding white façades, with rococo decorations' is not unlike the opening of *Red and Black* with its 'white houses with their steep, red tile roofs spread across a hillside'. It appears very much like the setting of a scene early in a novel—cf., for example, the opening of the 'Combray' chapter in *Swann's Way* where the first long sentence ends with '. . . an outline as scrupulously circular as that of a little town in a primitive painting.' Proust sees his setting as a painting; Simon finds it in a picture postcard. But Simon quickly introduces a distortion:

> The inking of the various colours does not precisely coincide with the contours of each of the objects, so that as a consequence the harsh green of the palm trees overlaps the blue of the sky, or the mauve of a scarf or a parasol encroaches on the ochre of the ground or the cobalt of the sea.

Thus he reminds us that we are looking not at a scene but at a postcard—at a *picture*: and that is a careful hint that that is all we shall do for the rest of the book and that that is all we do when we look; at the same time he shows us that the objects in our perception are not always clearly edged and flawless in the colour appropriate to them, they are not always what they are supposed to be, for it is not only on postcards that the colour of one object overflows into another.

The images which follow in the rest of the novel contain, in abstraction, the detailed themes of an old-fashioned romance; what in the latter might be a beautiful love affair is in *Triptych* a pornographic description, and what might be a portrait of bucolic life is a scattered imagery of earthy passions. But such an analysis, on which one could base an interpretation to please the reader who demands characters and action in a novel, seems irrelevant just as it would be irrelevant to say that a dark Rothko canvas represents the void. It is simply paint on canvas; and Simon's are simply words on the pages. No longer are we to be impressed by ideas; reality is a structure of an art form which is conscious of its own principles, which breaks up those principles which were formerly established and creates new ones, showing in the process that principles themselves are a foolishness of the mind while revealing that the new principles possess an immaculate logic. It is a beautiful confusion of form. Only *form*. The knowledge that we cannot know is exhilarating. The tongue licks the glans . . . so what? No one's life is going to change, no one is going to be made happier or sadder, it is merely words on a page, an event in the universe, a picture which flickers briefly in one's mind. The importance of the liberation effected by Simon's kind of writing has not been widely appreciated; it is a liberation from the lunacy of ideas.

In 'The Middle Years', a short story by Henry James, there is the suggestion that the sketchiest details of the objective world become transformed to a rich and believable reality when those details take on meanings projected by the imagination of a perceiver given to inventing fictions. At the start of the story, the main protagonist, a

novelist named Dencombe who is in his middle years and
who has been recuperating from an unidentified illness at
a hotel in Bournemouth, comes out for his morning stroll;
the postman, who happens to be passing by, delivers a
small parcel to him, taking which Dencombe proceeds to a
bench, his 'safe recess in the cliff.'

He postpones opening the parcel, being distracted by
seeing three persons on the beach: a young man, deeply
engrossed in a book as he walks, a 'large and mature' lady
who has about her an air of 'aggressive amplitude', and a
younger woman. Dencombe, who does not know them,
finds himself giving them probable identities: the older
woman is an 'opulent matron', the young man must be her
son, and the younger woman a 'humble dependent' of the
matron: the novelist in Dencombe makes up an instant
drama of their lives—the young woman surely 'nourished
a secret passion' for the man. 'Was that not visible from
the way she stole behind her protectress to look back at
him?' The novelist who makes people behave in certain
ways in order to suggest their emotions is witnessing
reality is if it were produced by a novelist: he is interpreting gestures and glances as he expects his readers to do
with similar fragments of behaviour in his own books.
Even from a distance, Dencombe can tell that the young
man is absorbed in a novel, and makes the observation,
seeing the disconsolate look on the young woman's face:
'while the romance of life stood neglected at his side he lost
himself in that of the circulating library.' Perhaps
Dencombe feels a glee that the young man should be
neglecting life for a fiction. The 'drama' surrounding the
three people that the novelist's mind has invented quickly
exhausts itself, and Dencombe opens his parcel which
contains an early copy of his latest novel, *The Middle Years*.
He is unable to look beyond the 'meretricious' cover, and
remembers the depression which had set in after he had
revised the final proof—'he had become conscious of a
strange alienation. He had forgotten what his book was

about.' His new novel is in his hands, but 'He couldn't have chanted to himself a single sentence, couldn't have turned with curiosity or confidence to any particular page.' He is filled instead with an overwhelming despair, with 'the sense of ebbing time, of shrinking opportunity' and the terrible feeling that though he had done his best, 'yet hadn't done what he wanted.' His illness and his depression come from the secret conviction that he has failed himself. It is the common condition of the novelist.

Chekhov: 'Everything I've written to date is nonsense compared with what I would like to have written and would be overjoyed to be writing.'

Tolstoy: 'What I have published in the past I consider a mere trial of the pen, a rough draft; what I am publishing now, although I like it more than my previous work, still seems weak—as an introduction is bound to be. But what's to follow will be—tremendous!!!'

Conrad: 'The *Outcast* is a heap of sand, the *Nigger* a splash of water, *Jim* a lump of clay.'

André Gide: 'If I were to disappear right now, no one could suspect, on the basis of what I have written, the better things I still have to write.'

And Virginia Woolf, after she has published *The Waves*: 'Oh yes, between 50 and 60 I think I shall write out some very singular books, if I live. I mean I think I am about to embody at last the exact shapes my brain holds.'

A writer's every attempt, as Eliot says in *Four Quartets*, is 'a different kind of failure', and a feeling of self-disgust aroused by a contemplation of one's own past work is most poignant when one sees one's latest book. That is Dencombe's situation to whom the thought that he might never write again is 'as violent as a grip at his throat.' But like other novelists, when Dencombe at last begins to glance at the pages of his latest novel he is pleased with some of the things he sees in it. He congratulates himself on his own art and laments the fact that no one else will see his art according to his own perception of it. There are still difficulties, and if he only had another chance, he would overcome those too and produce a magnificent work. He observes how his art has taken shape and reflects upon the slowness with which the flowering has begun to occur. A writer spent his life in learning to arrive at his art; one needed a second life in which 'to fructify'. It is a moment when Dencombe has a vision of the power he still has: it is the writer's illusion, after his despair has been a little alleviated by discovering a few striking sentences in his latest book, that he has within him the potential to create a masterpiece.

It is in this moment that the three persons on the beach reappear before Dencombe's consciousness. They had vanished from view because they had been coming up the path to the cliff. The older woman sits next to Dencombe on his bench in order to rest herself while her two companions stand nearby. Dencombe notices that the young man's book has a cover the same colour as his own, and soon each recognizes that it is indeed the same book. From the dialogue between the three people, Dencombe learns that the older woman is a Countess, the younger who attends her is Miss Vernham, and the young man Doctor Hugh. Dencombe is fascinated by what he hears, for his imagination is converting the three lives into the characters of a fiction; the novelist in him has suddenly become activated, and it is significant that just when he should be converting life to a fiction he 'already felt better of his melancholy'.

After escorting the ladies away, Doctor Hugh returns and strikes up a conversation with Dencombe without knowing that he is the celebrated novelist. Each tacitly assumes the other to be a reviewer, and Doctor Hugh says, '*Do* say, if you have occasion to speak of it, that it's the best thing he has done yet!' Dencombe is, of course, thrilled and does not reveal his identity.

If the young man had begun to abuse him he would

have confessed on the spot to his identity, but there was no harm in drawing out any impulse to praise.

What one begins to see in Doctor Hugh is that he is the representation of the ideal reader; the novelist who has been sitting lamenting that no one fully understands his art is being visited immediately by one who does, and is really only a projection of the novelist's mind: life does not give him the ideal reader and so he invents one for himself. While the story is realistic, James does give several hints to indicate that the reality we are witnessing is only taking place in the mind of the novelist who, because of the conditions attending the completion and publication of his latest work, is in an agitated state of mind in which he is particularly receptive to fantasies. Doctor Hugh 'became for poor Dencombe a remarkable, a delightful apparition.' He 'seemed to have been sent' for Dencombe's 'deep refreshment'. The word 'apparition' is again used later to describe Doctor Hugh to whom Dencombe says towards the end of the story 'You've made me think it all a delusion.' Also, early in the story, the sentence which originally presents the three characters on the beach, begins: 'His postponement associated itself vaguely, after a little, with a group of three persons . . .'. It is an *association* of ideas. The writer, reluctant to open the parcel which he knows contains his latest book, and filled, as he postpones the dreaded event, with emotions and ideas to do with his own sense of failure and potential for greatness, despairing that no one understands his art, begins to comfort himself with the fantasy of the ideal reader. The novelist's own habit of creating the illusion of reality in the minds of the readers of his fictions is having the effect of making him believe in his own illusion. In order that his illusion may not appear too unbelievable even to himself, the projected reality in which the novelist invests it is therefore made more complex by his instinct for inventing the details of life. The Countess and Miss

Vernham are invented to make Doctor Hugh more believable. Still, there are enough suggestions to make one wonder about the reality of Doctor Hugh. The Countess had 'picked him up at an hotel' in Switzerland: one would think that a Countess taken ill on a journey abroad is likely to send for the best doctor instead of picking up 'a practitioner without patients and whose resources had been drained dry by his studies'. That objection can possibly be answered by the notion that the Countess was perhaps a very eccentric person, or that her illness was too minor for her to be concerned about the reputation of the doctor. But a person who only recently has been 'drained dry by his studies' cannot have had the opportunity to read so widely in literature to· have the kind of astute literary perception which Doctor Hugh possesses. He is an apparition, and therefore too strongly present in Dencombe's mind. When Dencombe falls desperately ill, 'his doctor, the real one, the one who had treated him from the first' attends on him; the phrase, 'the real one,' is quietly inserted in a longish sentence, and it must imply that the other doctor who continues to see him, Doctor Hugh, is the unreal one. When Miss Vernham, playing the role of the anti-muse, comes to tell him that he must no longer see Doctor Hugh, 'after this Dencombe was certainly very ill.' His fondest creation is being taken away from him. His real doctor advises him 'to cultivate calmness and try, if possible, not to think'. After the one thing which has given him a new sense of life, the ideal reader, is to be denied him, the writer's fever is seen to reside in his brain; his doctor insists that he should 'take Doctor Hugh off his mind'. The Countess, Miss Vernham and Doctor Hugh go away to London. The novelist is abandoned and close to death, but a couple of days later Doctor Hugh returns bringing to the dying writer 'the great review of *The Middle Years*'. It is significant that Doctor Hugh should be the messenger of the novelist's moment of triumph; the review is 'an acclamation, a reparation, a critical attempt to place the author in the niche he had fairly won'. It is perhaps the novelist's final fiction, the erection of himself as a monument. For Doctor Hugh, Dencombe's art is a 'pearl'; but the poor novelist who had earlier observed that even his ideal reader had missed his intention and had wondered 'who in the world *would* guess it', sighs and says, 'The pearl is the unwritten—the pearl is the unalloyed, the *rest*, the lost!' That is the novelist's ultimate despair: the words he puts down on his pages will never match that notion in his mind of a beautiful thought expressed in an exquisite style and emerging in an astonishingly perfect form. He can only long for the unattainable, like Gide:

> The craft, I wish, may it be so discreetly original, so mysterious, so hidden, that it can never be seized in itself! I should like no one to be aware of me save by the perfection of my sentence and, because of that alone, no one able to imitate it.

The pearl is also reality: it cannot be written about in any comprehensive sense; it is the paradox of language that it has to leave a lot unwritten. At the start of the story, James says about Dencombe:

> He sat and stared at the sea, which appeared all surface and twinkle, far shallower than the spirit of man. It was the abyss of human illusion that was the real, the tideless deep.

Reality offers surfaces which we cannot penetrate but it stimulates our perception; the enormity of the sensations before us at any given moment is overwhelming: and so, we keep things in perspective, as the common phrase is, by interpreting reality within the narrow framework of a language which treats of exclusive categories. When Dencombe opens his book and begins to read it, James notes:

He dived once more into his story and was drawn down, as by a siren's hand, to where, in the dim underworld of fiction, the great glazed tank of art, strange silent subjects float.

The action of reading is seen as an immersion into a watery underworld; the image is carefully constructed to suggest an association with the earlier image of the sea. The 'surface and twinkle' of reality, it is implied, *can* be penetrated; but only by diving into the 'underworld of fiction'.

'The Middle Years'—a story by Henry James about the author of a novel called *The Middle Years*. 'The Garden of Forking Paths' is a story by Borges in which the ancestor of the main character has written a novel called *The Garden of Forking Paths* and 'The Garden of Forking Paths' appears in a section of stories given the general title THE GARDEN OF FORKING PATHS in a book called *Ficciones* of which THE GARDEN OF FORKING PATHS is one of two sections. Thus, what is said about *The Garden of Forking Paths* by the characters discussing it can apply also to 'The Garden of Forking Paths' as well as to THE GARDEN OF FORKING PATHS.

Certain realities are only to be perceived in carefully placed mirrors, and if the reflection before our contemplation is ablaze with a riot of brilliant images it is probably because the angle of the light in that moment excludes all shadows.

But a shadow can fall across the mind when that significant word which could, we are convinced as long as the word continues to elude us, bring that meaning to the brilliant images which would induce a sense of astonishing revelation, remains out of the mind's reach. Our failure to formulate a language which is a sufficiently illuminating equivalent of deeply felt emotions, or vague recognitions of inexpressible meanings, can become a source of anxiety.

Early in Virginia Woolf's *Between the Acts*, there is this description:

> The nurses after breakfast were trundling the perambulator up and down the terrace; and as they trundled they were talking—not shaping pellets of information or handling ideas from one to another, but rolling words, like sweets on their tongues; which as they thinned to transparency, gave off pink, green and sweetness.

Language provides neither information nor ideas; what the nurses are saying is of no interest, it is the usual gossip, the usual chatter, the usual filling of the air with sound: they are merely uttering words as sounds that recognizably belong to a species of creation without uttering meaning. A little later in the book there is this passage:

> Across the hall a door opened. One voice, another voice, a third voice came wimpling and warbling: gruff—Bart's voice; quavering—Lucy's voice; middle-toned—Isa's voice. Their voices impetuously, impatiently, protestingly came across the hall, saying: 'The train's late'; saying: 'Keep it hot'; saying: 'We won't, no, Candish, we won't wait.'

First, three voices enter; then each is given an adjective and then an adverb while each tone and pitch is identified with a particular character; finally, three statements are made, but the context gives the statements an appearance of generality: it is something they must have said a thousand times, repeating a formula of speech, for they are the phrases of people who will seize upon the tritely repetitive instruction—'Keep it hot'—with great facility but are incapable of using language in any real personal context. Language has become a collection of hackneyed quotations in their minds:

'She walks in beauty like the night,' he quoted.

Or:

'So we'll go no more a-roving by the light of the moon.'

(The second quotation is followed by: 'Isa raised her head. The words made two rings, perfect rings, that floated them, herself and Haines, like two swans down stream.' Words are often seen to have a physical presence; the air seems to be charged with them; the characters see them on one another's lips even when nothing is said). The characters repeat similar old quotations, nursery rhymes, street songs, and other half-remembered fragments from an earlier time; but they do not commit themselves to a speech which would reveal themselves, they do not use a language which would expose their emotions.

The action takes place on one summer's day at Pointz Hall, the country residence for over a hundred years of the Oliver family. Bartholomew Oliver, its oldest member, can only utter well-worn idioms or proverbs or bits of Romantic poetry. His widowed sister, Lucy Swithin, longs to see a harmony in the world, but words confuse her; she has been reading an Outline of History which informs her that in prehistoric times wild beasts roamed among the giant rhododendrons at Piccadilly, but for her it is only an amazing sort of information, without meaning. Then there is Bartholomew's son, Giles, and his wife, Isa, who do not say a single word to each other. A woman named Mrs Manresa, referred to as 'the wild child', and her friend William Dodge, 'the silent guest', drop in when the Oliver family is about to sit down for lunch. Mrs Manresa is talkative but in a vulgar sort of way, saying nothing of any importance. During the afternoon, the annual pageant takes place at Pointz Hall; a dramatised history of England, written and produced by a woman named La Trobe, is presented: the air is filled with words and though the Rev. Streatfield provides the audience of the neighbouring gentry and villagers with an interpretation at the end they all go away asking what it meant. La Trobe, the writer who has constructed a language in order to reveal experience, cannot bring meaning to her audience and even her desperate ploy at the end of her drama when in order to show the audience its own time she abandons words and makes all her characters on the stage hold up mirrors to the audience merely serves to baffle and annoy the gentle people gathered on the terrace on a fine summer's day.

There is also the figure of Rupert Haines, the man in grey, who does not utter a single word. Isa feels that she is in love with him but does not go beyond the fantasy of meeting him in the circumstances in which she had met Giles. The tension in her life is excruciating, but she cannot speak the words which would relieve it. Giles, too, finds his situation suffocating, but does not talk about it. These, and several of the other characters, are on the edge of an abyss which is a vast darkness of words. They are terrified of falling into it. The absence of language keeps their world secure although the tensions engendered by the silence, which they try desperately to relieve by repeating the familiar fragments, keeps them on another edge, that of total nervous collapse. They are lost, doomed; the perfect civilized order of Pointz Hall which has remained unthreatened for over a century has suddenly become fragile. More than the private despair of its occupants threatens the peace; it is June 1939, people have already begun to be killed in Europe, and twelve aeroplanes fly over during a pause in the pageant, making some in the audience wonder dimly if there is not some menacing meaning in their flying over a scene which so far has confirmed their sense of solid tradition.

The novel begins with the sentence

It was a summer's night and they were talking, in the big room with the windows open to the garden, about the cesspool.

The simplicity of the sentence is beautifully deceptive; on the surface it is only the conventional talk of neighbours, a discussion of a parochial event which gives people something to talk about without having to enter each other's lives; but the sentence contains a thought central to the novel: here are people surrounded by a garden, using words to talk when they do not wish to use a language which might reveal their emotions, talking what is more about a *cesspool* without realizing the symbolic awfulness of that word, for they are themselves the inhabitants of a cesspool.

The last sentence of the novel is simply the two words: 'They spoke.' At the end of the day, Isa and Giles have been left alone and must at last confront each other. And so, 'They spoke.' We shall never know if they really found the courage to say anything; it is more likely that they used words but avoided a language, that their passions remained suppressed and their feelings towards each other unspoken.

The opening talk about the cesspool does not go beyond a few lines. 'What a subject to talk about on a night like this!' one of the characters says. 'Then there was silence; and a cow coughed;' and a paragraph later, 'A bird chuckled outside.' Repeatedly, there is a withdrawal from words, and variations on the phrase, 'Then there was silence' ('The words died away.' 'But no one spoke.' etc.), appear like a refrain in the novel.

There is to be the pageant in the afternoon, and Isa hears the dialogue concerning it between Bart Oliver and his sister Lucy. 'Every summer, for seven summers now, Isa had heard the same words; about the hammer and the nails; the pageant and the weather.' They do not see that their lives consist of passing the days by repeating the phrases appropriate to the particular day. The three of them look out to see what the weather is doing. It is variable, as had been forecast. They see the sun and then the clouds which obscure it. And then each is aware that

> Beyond that was blue, pure blue, black blue; blue that had never filtered down; that had escaped registration. It never fell as sun, shadow, or rain upon the world, but disregarded the little coloured ball of earth entirely.

It is a rare moment of awareness. Perhaps there is God there, or perhaps they have had a glimpse of the universe which is indifferent to their lives. But their words turn away from the moment of revelation. Mrs Swithin says:

> 'It's very unsettled. It'll rain, I'm afraid. We can only pray,' she added, and fingered her crucifix.
> 'And provide umbrellas,' said her brother.

Fortunately, Isa's children are passing across the lawn, providing them with the more comfortable topic of how the boy is growing up and the baby shows no signs of measles, and they no longer need to look up at the blue. The threat of having to understand has passed.

Two pictures hang in the dining-room, one of them an ancestor of the Olivers from the eighteenth century, the other of an unknown lady bought because Bart Oliver liked the picture. Here then is history and civilization, a solid presence of the family's past and a work of art. But the room is

> Empty, empty, empty; silent, silent, silent. The room was a shell, singing of what was before time was; a vase stood in the heart of the house, alabaster, smooth, cold, holding the still, distilled essence of emptiness, silence.

But the people who come to dine there are not given this

perception. For them, the pictures are a conversation piece, a handy resource, something to tell an amusing anecdote about in order to fill up the silence. And that is precisely what happens when the family comes in to lunch and finds that unexpected visitors, Mrs Manresa and William Dodge, have just dropped in. Bart Oliver tells the anecdote to the visitors:

> 'That,' he indicated the man with a horse, 'was my ancestor. He had a dog. The dog was famous. The dog has his place in history. He left it on record that he wished his dog to be buried with him.'

Giles Oliver has returned from town and after lunch they all go out to have coffee in the garden, sitting in a semi-circle so that they may all enjoy the view. Figgis's Guide Book (1833) had commended the view which now in 1939 had not changed from that time.

> If Figgis were here now, Figgis would have said the same. So they always said when in summer they sat there to drink coffee, if they had guests. When they were alone, they said nothing.

'Beautiful,' said Mrs Manresa, 'beautiful . . .' but she cannot find any other words and begins to light a cigarette. A conversation about literature and art is attempted, but all that comes to their minds are the familiar quotations from Shakespeare and Keats.

> 'We haven't the words—we haven't the words,' Mrs Swithin protested.

No one realizes how anguished that cry is. A little later, Isa, looking at her husband, has a thought but 'not knowing what to say, abruptly, half purposely, knocked over a coffee cup.'

That, however, is the extent of the violence she can commit to express something of the rage within her. The thought passes her mind that 'somewhere surely one sun would shine and all, without a doubt, would be clear.' It is the absence of that illumination and the persistence of the doubt which contribute to her rage, but she does not pursue the thought, being distracted by the sounds of laughter coming from the actors getting ready for the pageant the proceeds from which are ironically to go to 'the illumination of our dear old church'—the Rev. Streatfield's extravagant phrase for installing electricity.

The audience assembles, but the pageant is a little delayed.

> There was nothing for the audience to do. Mrs Manresa suppressed a yawn. They were silent. They stared at the view, as if something might happen in one of those fields to relieve them of the intolerable burden of sitting silent . . . .
>
> The heat had increased. The clouds had vanished. All was sun now. The view laid bare by the sun was flattened, silenced, stilled.

Here they are, entirely illuminated! But there is nothing to say. They can only fidget, or suffer an immense oppression from one another's presence. All they can do is stare at the view, each in his own silence, until Mrs Manresa exclaims 'What a view!'

> Nobody answered her. The flat fields glared green yellow, blue yellow, red yellow, then blue again. The repetition was senseless, hideous, stupefying.

Again that blue, that overwhelming and indifferent universe; and the image presented by Woolf is of a helpless mankind trapped into becoming an audience of it, gaping at the void whose senselessness it would rather not have to think about. They cannot take it. Mrs Swithin decides to show William Dodge the house—the confining rooms with their pictures and furniture will be less oppressive than this empty space. Bart falls asleep in his chair.

The pageant finally begins. The ambitious Miss La Trobe is going to present the whole of British history, she is going to show them where they have come from and who they are. It is all very amateur and jolly, of course, but just as the view should have brought an illumination to those who gaped stupidly at it so the pageant, a crude literary enterprise, is to bring meaning to them. After the first act, the audience disperses, making for the Barn where tea is served, leaving Miss La Trobe to reflect upon her success. 'Hadn't she, for twenty-five minutes, made them see? A vision imparted was relief from agony . . .' But no one has witnessed her vision. 'She hadn't made them see. It was a failure, another damned failure! As usual.' Language, the symbols of the race, a memory of origins: nothing has revealed. The cup of tea is more important.

On his way to the Barn, Giles sees a snake lying choked with a toad in its mouth. 'The snake was unable to swallow; the toad was unable to die.' Here is the perfect representation of the predicament of all the characters. They are denied wholeness and they are denied death. They are obliged to endure a terrifying silence. Giles raises his foot and stamps upon the two creatures.

The mass crushed and slithered. The white canvas on his tennis shoes was bloodstained and sticky. But it was action. Action relieved him.

It is the same as his wife knocking off the coffee cup; he has been sitting staring at the empty blue of the fields and then listening to La Trobe's words; his little violent action is not calculated to relieve the agony of the snake and the toad but the one within himself.

The Barn reminds people of a Greek temple. But before they enter it, there is this description:

> The Barn was empty. Mice slid in and out of holes or stood upright, nibbling. Swallows were busy with straw in pockets of earth in the rafters. Countless beetles and insects of various sorts burrowed in the dry wood. . . . Minute nibblings and rustlings broke the silence.

On the one hand the allusions to classical architecture with which people impress one another, showing off their learning and experience, and on the other the reality of the continuing devastation. The silence which everyone is trying to break with neat little snippets of conversation is already being broken; the solid world of their tea and cakes is steadily and senselessly disintegrating. 'What delicious tea!' they exclaim although it tastes 'like rust boiled in water,' using words only to keep social pretences going.

Later in the pageant there is a chorus chanting, '*All passes but we, all changes . . . but we remain forever the same . . .*' and continues to declaim about the palaces and great kings and queens who have passed away. But

> The words died away. Only a few great names—Babylon, Nineveh, Clytemnestra, Agamemnon, Troy—floated across the open space. Then the wind rose, and in the rustle of the leaves even the great words became inaudible; and the audience sat staring at the villagers, whose mouths opened, but no sound came.

Once again, at the moment of truth a distraction, the accident of the wind rising, takes the words away. A revelatory language is made dumb. But in the silence which follows the cows in the fields begin to bellow.

> From cow after cow came the same yearning bellow. The whole world was filled with dumb yearning. It was

the primeval voice sounding loud in the ear of the present moment.

The audience does not recognize that the dumb yearning is its own, for it does not hear the 'primeval voice' in the cries of the cows. The pageant continues. A rain shower falls. 'O that our human pain could here have ending!' Isa murmurs, not intending to be heard. The rain stops. 'O that my life could here have ending,' Isa murmurs but takes care not to move her lips lest anyone should read her despairing thought. The actors jump out of the bushes, leaping, jerking, skipping, holding up mirrors to the audience, showing it a surreal imagery of itself. Fragments of faces in mirrors. The pageant ends.

The pageant ends and the Rev. Streatfield rises to give a summation, an interpretation, but his opening words are 'lost', for the breeze has risen and is rustling the leaves. The novel has almost ended, but as at its beginning where a cow's coughing filled in a silence, something in nature continues either to suppress words or to offer a distraction from their absence. The Reverend offers an innocent enough interpretation, his proper aim being to thank everyone concerned. In the middle of his ramblings, one of his words is cut in two: '. . . opp . . .' he says when 'Twelve aeroplanes in perfect formation like a flight of wild duck came overhead.' He pauses and continues, '. . . portunity . . .' In another pause a little later, 'Every sound in nature was painfully audible; the swish of the trees; the gulp of a cow; even the skim of the swallows over the grass could be heard. But no one spoke.' There is general embarrassment, but once more a trite, familiar event, uttering its own words, saves the day: the noise of the gramophone is heard, there is a roll and a flutter: '*God* . . . (they all rose to their feet) *Save the King.*' The convention proves to be merciful both to the actors and to the audience. At least one knows what to do without needing to exercise one's thought. The jolly old tune is awfully comforting. It guarantees that the event is really over. Now everyone can disperse, chatting away. About crepe soles. 'They last much longer and protect the feet.' About falling attendances in church. 'There's the dogs, there's the pictures.' Someone talks of science. 'The very latest notion, so I'm told is, nothing's solid.' The last statement ought to startle someone, but no one actually listens, for it is all talk to fill up the time before each finds his car and goes home.

The family is left alone except for Miss La Trobe who, gathering her things, has the glimmer of an idea for a new play. She wonders 'What would the first words be?' But: 'The words escaped her.' She walks away to a pub and there, drinking and smoking, finding herself imbued with a sense of creation, 'She heard the first words.' We do not know what they were, but can guess that they no more brought illumination to her audience than had her pageant. Back at Pointz Hall, Mrs Swithin returns to her Outline of History, Bart Oliver has fallen asleep (and is talking in his sleep, though all he mutters is 'Tinker, tailor, soldier, sailor,'—words without meaning), and Isa and Giles at last confront each other.

Then the curtain rose. They spoke.

The pageant of reality is about to begin; but the novel ends.

One senses that the characters are like the living dead in Eliot's *The Waste Land* where, too, literature has become fragments of familiar quotations and a meaningful language is lost to the tribe which will not recover from its malaise until the word has been restored. But these are people waiting for no form of regeneration; their real despair is that they do not know why they suffer. Isa might believe that she no longer loves her husband and that she longs for Haines and that this catastrophe of feelings that threatens to break up her marriage is the source of her misery; and Giles, feeling a passing infatuation for Mrs Manresa, might suffer from a despair as acute as his wife's: but neither realizes that the source of the despair is abstract, that their fate is to hang as two pictures on the wall, at best, and be someone's ancestors. Isa has seen the blue of eternity; Giles is disturbed by the tragedy shaping up in Europe. Both have a sense of utter annihilation, spiritual and physical; but each turns away from the words with which those thoughts must be confronted, and, understanding that there is a problem that has to be faced, makes the strain in the marriage the problem, reduces the larger question of existence to the pettiness of the self. And that, of course, is the only level at which most people can tolerate reality: their existence is only a matter of finding compromises with which to accommodate each other. And yet these people have moments when their sense of reality goes beyond the immediate and trivial circumstances of personal relationships, and they see the striking blue beyond the sun and the clouds; but all they can do is to stifle it: for language fails them; knowing only the trite phrases of the tribe, they do not have the words with which to arrive at a liberating meaning.

In its treatment of unexpressed emotion, *Between the Acts* anticipates some of the early films of Michelangelo Antonioni, and some too of Ingmar Bergman—those like *L'Avventura* or *The Silence* in which the characters are on the verge of speech but say nothing or utter some banality. And, of course, modern drama has made the failure of language a whole province of human action.

Those novelists whose imaginations have been driven to seek out, and attempt to establish, a reality more deeply revelatory of some vision than can be comprehended by a duller perception have made some of their characters into artists. Patrick White's Alf Dubbo in *Riders in the Chariot* (and, to a lesser extent, Hurtle Duffield in *The Vivisector*),

Wilson Harris's Da Silva da Silva in *Da Silva da Silva's Cultivated Wilderness*, and Virginia Woolf's Lily Briscoe in *To the Lighthouse* are people with an uncommon dimension of perception; one might call them visionaries. In each case, the writer is trying to invent a language which would be a verbal representation of a perception concerned only with form and colour: a change of lens from wide-angle to fish-eye on the same camera. The attention to pictorial representation as it emanates from the artist's possessed imagination is bizarre or abstract or surreal in the passages focusing upon the artist's struggle with his vision, for in these passages the writer has no obligation to the reality of the surfaces of things. In White, the pictures are meaningless to the other characters in the novel or worthy only of their derision. Harris's artist is already possessed of an other-vision while Lily Briscoe must struggle with the torment of not being able to transfer to the canvas what she believes she has seen, because the technique of a fashionable painter confounds her and the lives of the people around her are a vexing distraction, until, at the end, her vision and her canvas coincide.

The artist has her vision but it must inevitably remain inaccessible to the reader who has not seen the picture but only read a novel. There are intuitions to be grasped; the transformation, for example, of the whole novel as a vision in the reader's mind may or may not be effected; and, more often than not, the audience looking for a familiar wisdom turns, as from Kafka's hunger artist, to gape at the vivid beasts. The artists' visions may remain confined to the surface of the canvas, appearing as a swirling brilliance of colour or a flat, nearly colourless emptiness, their proper intensity never escaping the visionary's imagination, for any transmission must involve a loss of the original force, but a reader, coming to a written conception of the vision, can only have a remote sense of it. One has a memory of pictures as a reference but never the immediate and complete experience of a vision that any particular picture might have contained. Whatever the final spiritual tranquility induced in his mind by Dubbo's painting of the two Marys, the reader's gratification is not that he sees his vision, which the reader cannot in spite of the words painting it, but that the character whose existence has evinced a keen sympathy should at last reach a state of serenity.

But sometimes a novelist will make a reference to a painting the reader might have seen at a gallery to suggest a deeper level of understanding, as Beckett does in parenthesis of Watt: '(His resemblance, at that moment, to the Christ believed by Bosch, then hanging in Trafalgar Square, was so striking, that I remarked it.)'

At that point in *Watt*, Watt has become a mirror image of Sam, perhaps a suggestion that a novelist's character is only the projection of a figment of himself.

> Then I placed his hands, on my shoulders, his left hand on my right shoulder, and his right hand on my left shoulder. Then I placed my hands, on his shoulders, on his left shoulder my right hand, and on his right shoulder my left hand. Then I took a single pace forward, with my left leg, and he a single pace back, with his right leg (he could scarcely do otherwise).

A mirror image can scarcely do otherwise. And thus held by Sam, Watt begins to walk backwards and as he walks, 'so now he talked, back to front.' His first statement begins with '*Day of most, night of part, Knott with now.*' The words have no significance for Sam until he understands the rule of inversion employed in the construction of the sentences. Watt then changes the rule and begins 'to invert, no longer the order of the words in the sentence, but that of the letters in the word.'

> *Ot bro, lap rulb, krad klub. Ot murd, wol fup, wol fup. Ot niks, sorg sam, sorg sam. Ot lems, lats lems, lats lems. Ot gnut, trat stews, trat stews.*

These sounds make no sense to Sam until he grasps the rule, but no sooner does he begin to follow than Watt again alters the procedure. He begins 'to invert, no longer the order of the letters in the word, but that of the sentences in the period.' Watt changes the rules eight times, introducing a new complexity each time Sam has begun to understand his peculiar grammar. His final form of discourse does not employ the rules of inversion established, and now clearly comprehended by Sam, in the seven previous stages of the language he has been developing; but now, says Sam:

> in the brief course of the same period, now that of the words in the sentence, now that of the letters in the word, now that of the sentences in the period, now simultaneously that of the words in the sentence and that of the letters in the word, now simultaneously that of the words in the sentence and that of the sentences in the period, now simultaneously that of the letters in the word and that of the sentences in the period, and now simultaneously that of the letters in the word and that of the words in the sentence and that of the sentences in the period.

Sam can recollect no example of this final form of Watt's extraordinarily complex language. With each of the eight modes of speech invented by Watt, it takes Sam considerable time before he can grasp the rule and achieve a familiarity with its practice before he can understand what Watt is saying; and since his concentration is devoted entirely to discovering the rule being employed, he cannot even begin to look for a meaning in the speech; by the time he has discovered the rule and is ready to listen to sentences formed according to it, Watt has already begun to talk by a succeeding rule; and so, all that Sam has at the end are the eight different rules according to which Watt has put his sentences together; he has *understood* nothing other than the rules.

Thus the listener, hearing a flow of speech, which might contain an important truth, but being obliged to use all his concentration to unravel not the meaning but the grammar, is left in the end with the rules which permitted the peculiar combination of words, and receives no ideas from those words. Watt's final mode of speech is so complicated that were an example of it possible and the seeming anarchy of its grammar observed to be an exemplary adherence to principles, then perhaps a listener might witness some important truth. Or perhaps the listener would hear the gibberish of a madman.

The creation of a new grammar within a text using the words of a language which already exists is suggestive of the metaphor of words as mere sounds or at least primarily sounds; meaning becomes a function only of rules, understanding dawns when the rules have been discerned and seen to work in succeeding propositions; but that understanding is only of the grammar, not of what reality those words might seek to represent. Cf. Wittgenstein:

> When we first begin to *believe* anything, what we believe is not a single proposition, it is a whole system of propositions. (Light dawns gradually over the whole.)

Watt's inversions might each be an experiment to test the potential of language to see if it will not reveal a new meaning once its established rules are altered—just as a scientist will introduce variations into succeeding experiments when the solution continues to elude him—but no final revelation is to be had. Only a chaos of sounds fills the air, only a construction of sentences, and reality itself remains impenetrable beyond the structure of a grammar. Beckett in *Texts for Nothing I*:

> All mingles, times and tenses, at first I only had been
> here, now I'm here still, soon I won't be here yet, . . . I
> don't try to understand, I'll never try to understand any
> more, that's what you think, for the moment I'm here,
> always have been, always shall be, I won't be afraid of
> the big words any more, they are not big.

Times and tenses; past, present and future; and the words
are not big because they are only words.

Watt's experiments in grammar are perhaps a precur-
sor of Beckett's own later style where he dispenses with
punctuation and creates a language made up of phrases
which sound as though they are coming from a mouth
which is panting or grunting, as in *How It Is*. It is a rush of
words printed in blocks of paragraphs with the intermediate spaces suggestive of long durations of time, and
early in the novel it is suggested that here, too, the
speeches are to be locked within a structure of language:
'it comes the word we're talking of words I have some still
it would seem at my disposal'. When we use words, we're
talking of words, we make sentences possible; and if
anyone believes he understands ideas from those words,
then he is welcome to the fiction he has been so pleased to
imagine.

A man is crawling through mud. Perhaps it is an ocean
of mud, perhaps his entire universe is composed of mud;
he is not seen out of that element. His crawl is a slow
labour, the movement is that of one condemned to the
action: the compulsion does not come from an inner desire
but it is nevertheless a necessity. He must keep crawling
through the mud. He carries a sack, tied by a cord to his
neck, containing some tins and a tin opener. Each movement of his arms and legs as he pushes himself through the
mud could take a moment or years. He pants out strings of
phrases which could be rushing out of his mouth in a rapid
torrent or are being uttered, word after painful word, with
pauses of years between them. 'I say it as I hear it' he

repeats many times. Where do the words come from—memory, the air, the prompting author? They seem to be just *there*, a force of language spontaneously present in the universe.

The character in the first part of *How It Is* is crawling towards another, named Pim, who has preceded him and whom he reaches in the second part; by the third, and final, part he expects another character, Bom, to catch up with him as he has with Pim; but it appears that these three are only part of a chain of millions: humanity seems to have become trapped in a timeless zone in a silent universe of mud, but it cannot escape the tormenting knowledge of its own existence, each being condemned to crawl forever. At the end of the novel, the millions are reduced to one:

> and this business of a procession no answer this business of a procession yes never any procession no nor any journey no never any Pim no nor any Bom no never anyone no only me no answer only me yes so that was true yes it was true about me yes and what's my name no answer WHAT'S MY NAME screams good

There is not even the character that the novel began with; it is the author himself who is screaming, for the novel began with the words 'how it was I quote before Pim' and ends with 'how it was end of quotation after Pim how it is'. The entire novel, then, has been a quotation, which is to say a projection of words from one mind to another and, in the end, the other is not the character of the book but the reader. 'I say it as I hear it' are words which the reader is compelled to repeat, for, such is the force of Beckett's prose, the words have been heard rather than read, and if anyone is really panting out the words, it is the reader.

There is no question of an objective reality in *How It Is*. The universe of mud with its millions of bodies, or its one body, the universe which has become 'the incredible tohu-bohu', is only a field of consciousness where words occur with an obsessive force. If the character is tormented by the meaninglessness of existence, the screaming voice at the end is the author's and the tormented mind the reader's who has, in the final moments of the novel, come to the recognition that the author's despair is also his own. No images of reality have been necessary to create the idea; a broken language, which is itself tormented, has done so, and what one is left with is another fiction to ponder—which may or may not reveal some reality. We shall never know.

The novel begins with 'past moments old dreams . . . things always and memories'. It is to be the substance of all fictions, time past considered during time present, the little things taken up for scrutiny once again to see if they will not open up some secret. It is to be 'my life of moments', but immediately there is a problem: 'how I got here no question not known'—one has no knowledge of one's birth; one simply, suddenly, without knowing finds that one *is* and that one is *here*. The phrases begin to accumulate and to repeat themselves: 'I say it as I hear it' and 'vast stretch of time'—which in the course of the novel will become refrains or brief melodic phrases in a large discordant symphony. Suddenly a phrase,

something wrong there

appears in a paragraph all its own, and this too will be often repeated. It is a reflexive comment in the consciousness uttering the phrases, indicating sometimes that there is something wrong in the structuring of the previous thought and sometimes that there is something wrong in the order of the world which made such a thought possible. Although the character says 'I haven't been given memories this time', he does record images from his memory: there is a mother and a child, presumably there has been some obscure beginning to this life. Then suddenly

warmth of primeval mud impenetrable dark

words which announce the setting of the novel. There are moments when the character has a suspicion that everything has already happened:

this voice once quaqua then in me when the panting stops part three after Pim not before not with I have journeyed found Pim lost Pim it is over I am in part three after Pim how it was how it is I say it as I hear it natural order more or less bits and scraps in the mud my life murmur it to the mud

During his painful progress towards his future there is the heightened despair which comes from the thought that the imagery with which he anticipates it is not an invention of what might happen but a record of what has already taken place. Since he can only say it as he hears it, he may only be saying that which is spoken of events long past but spoken in such a way as to suggest that they are still to come. And although the organs of his life are no longer active, his consciousness continues to record perceptions, and even in the mud the details of a vivid imagery continue to be spoken.

The narrative takes on a poetical intensity with

you are there somewhere alive somewhere vast stretch of time then it's over you are there no more alive no more then again you are there again alive again it wasn't over an error you begin again all over more or less in the same place or in another as when another image above in the light you come to in hospital in the dark a paragraph which contains the essential idea of the novel: one has not died yet, one has merely reawakened in the dark with no knowledge other than the awareness of the continuation of one's existence, without knowing why it must be so, and one cannot rid oneself of the anguish which that desperate knowledge entails: even that which already should have happened is yet to occur. To exist is only to have the thought that one has not died just when there appeared to have been a termination of the self: a constant renewal of the awareness of that death is all. One is obliged to 'find something else to last a little more', somehow one must fill out the time which does not seem to have an end as the novelist must his pages, but 'time passes I remain', even after the stories have been invented and spun out, there is more time in which to be and one turns to 'these details in preference to nothing'.

But from time to time there are 'these sudden blazes in the head' which are 'like a handful of shavings aflame'—ideas, intuitions into how it is?—and when they appear with their sudden flames, 'the spectacle then'! But these are momentary glimpses which perhaps suggest that there has to be at least a potential for revelation; the illuminating perception, briefly glimpsed as one raises one's eyes from, say, the concrete pavement to the grimy bus whining past, may not be an illusion after all, but it goes so quickly that no words can grasp it and one is left staring at a point of light where one thought a flashing idea had come aflame, but it is only, one realizes at last, a point of red light at the back of the bus which is braking to a halt.

Beckett can only return to grammar:

a little less of no matter what no matter how no matter when a little less of to be present past future and conditional of to be and not to be come come enough of that on and end part one before Pim

This life we prize so much, it is only to do with the conjugation of a verb. And one's sympathy is drawn when Beckett's character says that he 'understood everything and forgave nothing', for whatever epistemological puzzles might continue to confound us the fact is that we do understand a great deal; even a vague comprehension of the rudiments of modern science comprises a considerable feat of having acquired some knowledge; but even a complete and a sophisticated possession of this knowledge which would entitle us to claim that we understand everything would be no help in answering the simple question: why? Learning remains an irrelevance; it is only an amusing way of passing the time. We cannot forgive learning for having failed us. That will not, and must not, stop the quest; but the more thorough the knowledge of the what and the where and the how the greater the resentment that we cannot know why. It is difficult not to agree with Beckett in part two of *How It Is*: 'let him understand who has a wish to I have none'. The knowledge which we already have is too terrible for us to want to wish for more. It is 'drivel drivel happily brief', it is 'little blurts midget grammar'—phrases which perfectly describe both Beckett's narrative style and his idea of human knowledge.

But the character must crawl on through the infinity of mud, murmuring the words which come to him, whispering his tragic monologue to the mud, for he must reach Pim sooner or later, another being in a situation more advanced than his in its physical decay but still alive though scarcely capable of expressing the pain it is continuing to endure.

He reaches Pim who is nearly lifeless, sunk in the mud on his belly, and by scratching words on his back, pounding his kidneys, driving a tin opener into his buttocks and thumping on his head he attempts to elicit some meaning from him. The character is determined to hear something from Pim: 'samples whatever comes remembered imagined' of his life above in the light. When Pim is finally taught to speak, he has a memory of his wife who fell from a window, or jumped from it, and is seen in hospital, like Malone in his bed, like Pim in the mud; the memory is from his 'life above'—from which one could surmise that the present life in the mud is a form of purgatory, that perhaps the character has died, perhaps Pim and Bom have died, but there has been no death, only an awful continuation, what stopped in the life above was not a death, it was only a transference from one horror to another. Pim has a few scattered memories, but in that life above 'never anyone never knew anyone always ran fled elsewhere some other place my life above places paths nothing else'. In the end, all Pim can do is to howl.

From there to the third part in which the character becomes like Pim, and another, Bem or Bom, will catch up with him and torment him as he has tormented Pim. There is a whole line of them, perhaps a million Pims and Boms, crawling from west to east at the rate of forty yards a year, crying aloud, or hearing words echoed in their minds, the words of 'drivel drivel' in 'midget grammar', a couple of phrases taking months in which to be expressed. Towards the end the language explodes out of the consciousness in which it has hitherto appeared, for suddenly there is the line

my life we're talking of my life

and the words which had been heard in the mind of the character crawling through the mud appear now to be expressed aloud by another voice, perhaps the author's (or perhaps the reader, recognizing that he could have been reading about himself, has begun to shout MY LIFE WE'RE TALKING OF MY LIFE!). Though the words within the character's mind return for several more paragraphs, the other voice, expressing its own anguish

and making a commentary on what has been said, keeps
intruding:

> cumulation of offices most understandable if it will be
> kindly considered that to hear and note one of our
> murmurs is to hear and note them all

is a statement in which 'our' refers to more than the
situation in which Pim and Bom find themselves; clearly,
the reader is being invited to make a general connection,
for we read a little later:

> and that linked thus bodily together each one of us is at
> the same time Bom and Pim tormentor and tormented
> pedant and dunce wooer and wooed speechless and
> reafflicted with speech in the dark mud nothing to
> emend there

Whereas many another group of words is qualified by the
phrase, 'something wrong there', there is 'nothing to
emend' in this paragraph. The closing half a dozen pages
of the novel, while again taking up the imagery of the mud,
have several similar statements, each with a definitive air
about it, in which a general commentary on how it is,
rather than a dramatic conclusion, is being offered. A new
phrase—'if it will kindly be considered'—and variations of
it, is used in the paragraphs which contain the generalisations, from which it must follow that the reader is being
invited to consider the evidence that he has been given.
There is a tranquility in the tone of these paragraphs, the
language does not have the panting, pained intensity of
the rest of the book: a calm seems to have set in:

> and if it is still possible at this late hour
> to conceive of other worlds

> as just as ours but less exquisitely organized

> one perhaps there is one perhaps somewhere merciful enough to shelter such frolics where no one ever abandons anyone and no one ever waits for anyone and never two bodies touch

We are invited kindly to consider such a proposition and its implications. But Beckett himself seems to have a doubt:

> if all that all that yes if all that is not how shall I say no answer if all that is not false yes

The brief calm ends with the realization that all that is indeed false. The voice that now explodes contains an intense rage:

> there was something yes but nothing of all that no all balls from start to finish yes this voice quaqua yes all balls yes only one voice here yes mine yes when the panting stops yes

One is left with the screaming voice—'DIE screams I MAY DIE screams I SHALL DIE screams'—but there is no answer from the silent universe, there is no end to the torment of existence; and nor is there any relief in the 'end at last', for it is only the end of part three and its final words, 'how it is', remind one of 'how it was', which has just been while one has been reading the novel and which are also the first words of the novel, so that the reader is left crawling in the infinite mud and cannot escape from the fiction which has told him nothing at all about reality but only created a new reality for him to endure.

A sentence which one has written and which appears to contain a neatly expressed thought often does so because its form resembles a sentence which impressed us in a writer we happened to have been reading. One's belief in one's own originality involves a lapse of memory: one forgets, for the moment, that the new thought has only sought to re-discover a language already lodged in the mind by another writer and, during one's forgetfulness, one's self-admiration is only an intenser admiration for that writer.

Sometimes when one attributes one's thought to another writer and confesses that the form of one's words is derived from his work, one is only being modest and entertains the secret hope that an impartial observer will one day do us justice and proclaim our originality.

I have no ideas but the combinations of words suggested by my brain sometimes convince me that I have arrived at an interesting observation. That the observation seems interesting is, however, a psychological error: I mistake the feeling of gratification which a new phrase gives me for a new insight.

We're not always responsible for our habits for they are sometimes an inheritance bestowed upon us by the tribe of which we are the members. And no tribe has a sense of its own identity without having an established body of prejudices. In the arts, for example, the most cultivated audiences are convinced that their admiration of Beet-

hoven or Brahms, Constable or Turner, Balzac or
Dickens is based entirely on their independent judge-
ment and would be outraged to be told that their opinion
is only a habit inculcated upon their minds by generations of agreement. Generally speaking, no one in
England takes more than two lumps of sugar with his
tea.

There are less than twenty years left of the twentieth
century and still most audiences cannot listen to the
music Webern composed in the first decade of the
century, considering it *too modern*. Nothing in science
is considered too modern; indeed, if science did not
come up with new discoveries it would cease to be taken
seriously by the very people who, when it comes to the
arts, behave as if they were the contemporaries of
Newton.

When a culture has not produced anything significantly
new for some time, it discovers in its past a period that
had been justly neglected: past mediocrity which once
enjoyed a vogue under a fancy label becomes a national
treasure and its rediscovery reassures the nation that it
is still discovering the new in art. E.g. the Pre-
Raphaelites in England.

I am listening at this moment to a piece by Stockhausen
which is constructed on some elaborate and strict
formal principles which are beyond the comprehension
of my untrained ear, but which to me is a music full of
surprises and unpredictable thrilling sounds, compris-
ing a beautiful sequence of aural sensations. How
boring it would be to be listening to some familiar Elgar
at this moment! And that is not to say that unfamiliarity

is an important element in one's enjoyment of music; rather, it is a statement about an intuitive response to a composer's principles, which may be obscure and yet engender within one a conviction of his seriousness and a desire to listen again from a new point of view in order to arrive, at some future stage, at a more complex enjoyment. To my ear, Stockhausen sounds as if he is creating music, Elgar as if he is going through the motions of putting together what he thinks music should be.

People who know nothing about an art pretend to a profound knowledge of it when they praise a lesser known artist, but whose name is generally, if vaguely known, comparing him favourably to one whose genius is universally applauded.

The condition of Robinson Crusoe—to be placed in a situation where the human being is obliged to evolve new strategies for survival. Has there been a hero in fiction who has not been in the same situation?

The only times I am *concerned* with reality is when I have to visit the doctor or the dentist—and these are occasions when I make a deliberate attempt to believe that the world is a fiction of which my pain is an imaginary event.

After a football or a cricket match is over, our discussion of it also dwells upon that which did not happen; we're thrilled by the conception in our imagination of what might have happened if a pass had been intercepted or a catch not missed: we convert the reality we have observed into a fiction and continue, long after the event, to elaborate an ever-changing plot. Our team *could* have won; or, it came *so near* to losing.

When one tells a lie which is accepted as truth, one understands that language is no different from paint, one's audience is only looking at colour.

G. E. Moore's proof of common sense has to be nonsense for the very simple reason that the 'I' who put up his right hand to show that a hand exists could well be a character in 'my' imagination, a magician capable of all sorts of tricks. There's no more unreliable narrator than 'I'.

When I read in a philosopher that a sentence with such and such a proposition cannot be true, I'm intrigued by the possibility of a whole body of untrue sentences; but then I realize that to utter truth is not the function of sentences, for sentences have only one purpose—to put words together according to grammatical principles. Truth is a function of interpretation and not of language: we *believe* something is true, we do not *know* that it is true. This is why fiction, which is indeed a body of untrue sentences, often leads one to have the conviction that one has apprehended truth.

Mrs Dalloway—what a glorious orgy of semi-colons! Interesting to note that some of the finest writers, like Virginia Woolf and James Joyce, while being radicals in technique are, indeed, the greatest conservatives in the language. You will not see them construct a sentence except on precise principles: correctness is important to precision, and without precision you cannot be taken seriously as a radical.

You have only to read the correspondence between Hopkins and Bridges to understand that men who enjoy a great literary reputation in their own time are sometimes significantly ignorant about literature, and not only that of their own time.

A writer who is neglected in his own time and is obliged to suffer the spectacle of witnessing his inferior contemporaries receiving praise and awards is comforted by the reflection that names such as Iliodor Palmin, Dmitry Grigorovich, Nikola Zlatovratsky, Ieronim Yasinsky and Tatyana Shchepkina-Kupernic were more important to some Russians than their contemporary, Chekhov. But neglect in one's own time is not a guarantee that one is a genius and instant praise is not a sign that one is not any good; like the Bible, literary history offers a variety of examples to fit the requirements of any fool whose vanity is so bruised that he needs to be comforted.

We are constantly trying to adjust ourselves to some new nuance in a confusion of opinions.

The professors of literature who have become the champions of popular culture and teach novels which possess a mass appeal have not been able to tell me why it is that if I want to see tennis, I prefer to watch the men's singles final at Wimbledon and not the game in progress between two middle-aged insurance agents in the public courts.

The more important English becomes as a world language, the more will its serious new literature be threatened. Unfortunately, the rest of the world is interested not in the language of England and America but in their consumer products. Soap, toothpaste and English-language paperbacks may now be bought at most international airports.

By the end of the nineteenth century both literature and science abandoned the world.

Newtonian physics can be grasped by any human eye and one appreciates Newton as one does Gainsborough, but Heisenberg is like an abstract painter, one can only understand him when one ceases to look at the world as it appears.

Did *art* exist before the twentieth century?

The poem I write tells me only that I am writing that poem, and if it contains the line, 'I wake and feel the fell of dark, not day', that is not a confession of the state of my feelings but only a line which my imagination has believed as possessing the kind of force that I want in the poem that I am writing. The line came from the conviction of the moment, a conviction to do with aesthetic belief and only partially with the state of my emotions. Were I writing at another time, the poem would be different, but *not* simply because my emotions would be different.

Why should I expect to know anything about myself through sentences of which I myself am the maker?

There is nothing more easy to contrive in writing than the surreal image: it is the favourite device of writers who would like to be considered avant-garde.

It is as easy to produce what passes for new writing as it is to produce a traditional novel which follows a commercially successful formula. What is difficult is to create a text which owes nothing to the pressures of trends but which seeks to discover thought; in short, the writer's struggle is not with his subject matter and not with form, but with style. Sometimes the struggle with style involves one in a prior struggle with form; never, however, with subject matter.

Novels whose subject matter is their greatest appeal are invariably vastly popular; they are the very ones which no one wants to read when popular concerns have taken a different direction. Novels which stand on the force of their style alone win their readers slowly, in little bands here and there, until the work becomes one of the layers which compose human consciousness.

That the majority of readers of contemporary fiction are more impressed by subject matter than by style explains why, among American novelists, Saul Bellow, who knows what to write about, is preferred to Thomas Berger, who knows how to write. Bellow is at once a psychologist, an anthropologist, a political commentator and a philosopher. Berger is a novelist, and nothing else. That is why Bellow appears important to intellectuals while Berger's most ardent admirers are some other novelists. And that is why twenty or thirty years from now Bellow will be one of those obscure funny names one sees who were mistakenly awarded the

Nobel Prize, like Pearl Buck, and Berger will be read seriously, like Henry James.

The taste of one's own time is always uncultivated.

What keeps a work alive is not its popularity with the public but that future generations of writers find it impossible to ignore it.

Galsworthy, Maugham, Waugh were ahead of their time. Had they lived some generations later, they would have been successful script-writers of television soap-operas, those names that roll by so quickly at the end of a television programme and do not even register in the viewer's consciousness.

My previous books would be better if I were to write them now but if they had not been written I would not now want to write them.

The fact that every writer believes that the book he wrote ten years ago would be better if he were to write it now implies that the further we are from our subject matter the better equipped we are to create the language which best suits that subject matter. This is why Flaubert said that the 'finest works are those that contain the least matter', why he wished to write a book about nothing, and Raymond Roussel very nearly did.

The best works are those whose ideas I do not immediately—and perhaps never will—understand but whose form continues to engage my interest and whose style gradually takes on the quality of a particular sensation, evoking, as precisely as the fragrance of mango-blossom, its own essential flavour, even in memory. To one who knows his work, simply the word *Racine* is enough to fill the body with a distinct pleasure.

Sometimes I've begun a new novel because a certain way of writing attracted me while composing my previous novel, which new form, however, did not suit the inner necessities of the work in progress so that I've had to invent a new work in order to satisfy an irrational craving to see what the new form looks like when it appears out of its own necessity in a context natural to it.

Art is a way of seeing; artistic expression is a speculative, formal way of seeing; one makes brush strokes according to a certain inclination and, once having acquired an attachment to that particular inclination, accords the resulting form a hypothetical seriousness to see if that will not shape the style with which the vagueness in one's mind becomes transformed to a concrete imagery: it has nothing whatever to do with representing truth, but the reality that gets created in the process may possess an interesting insight into a truth.

Good art, coming out of a particular time, sometimes has nothing to do with that time; but without it, that time would not be what we believe it is.

After seeing a play or hearing a concert, there is the

compulsion to talk. We discuss the performance with our friends, praising or criticising the acting or the costumes or the interpretation given to the piece. The person who comes up with a verbose criticism of the performance is considered a wit, and one who interprets it to evince from the production a meaning that had escaped us is considered brilliant. Few are prepared to admit that the best performance is that which leaves nothing to be said after it has been experienced.

'Let us be realistic!' we exclaim—meaning, 'Why don't you see my point of view?'

Unamuno says that we are a dream that God is having and that in order to ensure our existence it is necessary to keep God asleep: which we do, says Unamuno, by singing hymns and intoning prayers in a tone calculated to keep the listener asleep. But let us observe the reverse of this thought and say that God is a dream in our minds. He can only exist as long as we dream Him. This is why He has given us a fertile imagination, capable of making up a fantastic literature, so that He can appear as a hero in our fictions. And just to make sure that we continue to dream, He has given us tobacco, wine, alcohol, opium and, most importantly, a brain too easily impressed by ideological thought which we are convinced is an expression of universal truth.

A novelist created the world. And then, looking for a way of withdrawing from the responsibility, he created God. This is why God is perceived as being improbable, being an invention of a second-rate mind which could not come up with a convincing idea and so it came up with a wildly extravagant one in order to make up for implausibility. It's pure sensationalism, but that's what an undiscriminating audience likes.

God, not caring to accept responsibility for the world which had no godlike qualities to recommend it, handed it over to a committee of third-rate novelists since He realized that they were keen enough to take seriously the boredom, the repetition, the coincidences and the errors of mankind; and the reason why he decided to form a committee only of third-rate novelists is that He saw that they possessed in greater measure the qualities which motivated the invention of falsehood: vanity and envy.

I cannot believe in God; therefore, I think about Him every day.

The light from the table-lamp on my desk falls in such a way that it casts the desk's shadow across the floor, throwing a nearly black rectangle across the green carpet; to my right is a door painted in an off-white matt finish, and the light throws a soft reflection from the centre of the door. These are details which belong to my immediate everyday perception. There are many others—watching rain-drops fall from the eaves on to the ligustrum bushes where the drops make a sort of neon edge when they fall in quick succession on the leaves, or seeing a mocking-bird alight on a low branch of an oak tree when I put on the lawn sprinkler in hot weather and watching the bird make quick forays into the spray of water—and it is this kind of detail with which one's day is filled. You will not, however, be burdened with such observations of a character's reality in a novel. I have been cooking. My finger tips, when I hold them before my nose, exude what to me is a wonderful smell which comes from having chopped garlic, ginger and fresh coriander. No one knows this.

'Science fiction' is a slick label given to old stories set in a technological environment. Wine vinegar is still, and only, vinegar.

A translator needs no experience of life but an intimate experience of two languages and the poem he translates is removed from the original poet's experience and is now only a text which contains subtle problems of language the successful solution of which is the translator's principal preoccupation.

There are very few texts—whether of the shortest lyric or the longest novel—which have not undergone several revisions, deletions, additions, etc. Something of the writer's experience might be contained in the first draft but without the subsequent playing around with words or the testing of variations of lines of verse to see if they work or the interpolation of new episodes to make a fiction more interesting, without an intelligent fooling around in a confusion of words and without the curiosity to see if a new form cannot be extracted from the mess before one there is scarcely ever a work of art. The word *mess* is not lazily chosen. You've only to look at some of the manuscripts that exist of the greatest works.

The more a writer tries to perfect his work the more he is engaged in the possibilities of language and less with the idea with which he began.

I do not know why there should be schools of criticism or labels attached to certain types of critical thought. Criticism is only a changing point of view. It is the easiest language game to learn and has the advantage of allowing the player many strategies through which to make a show of wisdom. Flaubert wrote: 'It doesn't require much brains to be a critic'; Valéry: 'Criticism. The scrubbiest cur can inflict a fatal injury—it only has to be *mad*.' And Chekhov: 'I divide all works into two kinds: those I like and those I don't like. I have no other yardstick, and if you ask me why I like Shakespeare and don't like Zlatovratsky I shall have no answer.'

There has been a tendency among critics in the second half of the twentieth century to see themselves as apart from the art about which they write. They see themselves as creators in their own right, and sometimes give the impression that they would prefer it if the art itself were to disappear.

Most critics serve only the intellectual and emotional prejudices of their time, and even the rare ones with a larger understanding who—like F. R. Leavis, for example—are the teachers of a generation, whose taste and ideas they formulate, are seen with the passage of time to have been essentially stupid.

In the teaching of English literature, the highest paid positions are held by academics who have made a name for themselves as critics. There is a greater body of them now than ever before. What one fails to understand is why, at the same time, there is a greater body than ever before of the most abominable and trivial literature being produced, most of it by writers who went to a university and perhaps even took a course with the eminent critic with the endowed chair.

The study of a writer's sources is a particularly futile activity. When eating a mango, I have no interest in the soil from which it originated.

A writer's dreams and buried memories go into his novel along with the recognizably objective subject matter; the reader, finishing the novel, turns to his own dreams whose imagery may be coloured by the events of the novel. A writer does not always know what he has written and a reader does not always know what he has read. The unconscious imagery of one mind enters into the unconsciousness of the other; perhaps a recognition of an experience takes place; perhaps one is convinced by an elusive idea that one has seen the brilliant centre of some dazzling thought; but it is impossible to say exactly what one has understood.

Without *the new* any art is doomed, of course, but newness cannot be achieved without a price: it casts a curse on its time, for the great originator of a style is inevitably followed by a mob of imitators who can abstract his principles without possessing his quality of perception but who convince one another and their generation that they are producing a true art when they are only engaged in a shallow mimicry.

Seeing the house with its walled-in garden and hearing the voices of unseen people, who one imagines are inhaling perfumes of the rose and the honeysuckle, and being entranced by the laughter (which sounds sensuous, of course) of young females, one imagines not the life led by these invisible characters but the life one oneself could be leading there and rehearses an entire existence composed only of long summer evenings when one's self is suffused with the fulfilment of subtle passions.

My own reality is made bearable by the reality I posit for myself. I care less for what I am; and more for what I could become. The truth about my reality is mundane; but as a character in the fictions of myself I possess a fascinating complexity.

The *other!* Pirandello, Unamuno: each the other's *other*, which would be one way of reading their works! How obsessed were they with this terrible question.

Literature and Cultural Heritage: the United States inherited England's insularity and Europe's sense of being superior and exclusive. For years I've been telling my friends among American writers that Machado de Assis is a genius who simply must be read; not one has read him, however, but several of them have read Solzhenitzyn.

Literature and Geography: do the Pyrenees explain why English writers have historically known so little of the literature of the Iberian peninsula and, by extension, of Latin America?

Literature and Historical Habit: I've come across students who find it difficult to read a novel set in

Colombia or in Peru because 'all those Spanish names are confusing', but the same students are perfectly at home with Tolstoy and Chekhov.

Literature and Imperial Politics: few Englishmen, even among university professors, could name one each of an Urdu poet, a Sanskrit poet, a Bengali poet or a Punjabi poet. On the other hand, many an educated person in India and Pakistan will be able to rattle off a list beginning with Chaucer and ending with Tennyson—and a good many will come as far as Dylan Thomas who was alive when the Empire was dissolved.

A writer cannot be a royalist (although as a prince of language he is a leading aristocrat of his tribe) because he belongs to a cultivated, and not an inherited, nobility. But how one regrets the collapse of the aristocracy! The advance of the middle classes has been the advance of vulgarity. The greatest political invention of the human mind, democracy, is the greatest destroyer of human values. The quality of education has become trivial because the feeblest mind in the state must be guaranteed the illusion of having received it. The cheap best-seller passes for literature among the many. People must not be made to feel in any sense under-privileged and so the commonest aspects of the popular culture become the objects of a sham learning. Good art is threatened because the purchasing power of the great middle class increases each year.

Any new liberation, whether in the arts or in society, won through sacrifices or those forces of necessity which make a new movement inevitable, releases a new energy, after it has happened, among people of mediocre talent, so that the new freedom ends in the vulgarisation of the very thing that has been liberated. A new style in art, establishing an entirely fresh perspective through which all past art has to be re-evaluated and making the standard more rigorous than before, leads to the general lowering of the standard among the majority of artists who suddenly find a new, apparently easy opening into a world from which they had been excluded by the earlier, 'tyrannical' standard.

I am at present writing a novel and have finished about half of it. So far all I've tried to do has been to invent complex and nearly unbelievable relationships among several characters; in the rest of the book I shall have to try, without diminishing the reader's interest, to make the complex appear perfectly simple and the unbelievable perfectly credible. I have no idea how I shall achieve this, but I will since I've done so before. A solution always presents itself. Those who will praise the remarkable plot will never realize that all that a novelist does is to create difficulties for himself and then seek solutions for them. It has nothing to do with reality.

We create fictions because we do not know what happens after death. In short, we try to improve upon the fictions created by philosophy and religion which ascribe portentous meanings to life and assume for existence a significance which is entirely hypothetical. If there were to be a certainty of an after-life, then we would not have the obsession we do with reality because we would not, in that event, have the concept of any reality which was unreal. We would simply accept the present as a colourless fact. Does this imply that the idea of time depends on not knowing that which is not happening right now while one has the awareness that that which is not happening is precisely that occurrence of events which makes us think of the *present*?

What is so human about novelists is that they never give up hoping that their next book will make them very rich. I like looking at the picture in Balzac's biography of the manuscript first page of *Le Père Goriot* where after writing the title and a few lines, Balzac has filled the page with calculations of what look like his current debts and his royalty expectations from the new, unwritten book, and I like to think that he must have been convinced that this time he was going to come out ahead. What fills one with great excitement and optimism on starting a novel is the thought—which soon becomes a conviction and then a certain expectation—that this time one is bound to succeed, pay off all one's debts, and have surplus wealth left over to invest in real estate and stocks and shares with the income from which one will embark on a leisurely tour of the world, and before one can write the first sentence one spends two days looking at the travel agency brochures during which time of serious deliberation one resolves to spend at least one week at the Copacabana Palace Hotel in Rio de Janeiro. Tolstoy wrote in a letter: 'The point is I want to get as much money as possible for this work which I'm particularly fond of and which has cost me a great effort.'

The material world can be so comforting, the solid surfaces so reassuring. The family jewels continue to glitter even when the family is in disarray and the house of ambitious and pretentious construction, which may be named 'Xanadu' or 'Kudjeri', has begun to decay. We can walk across the firm lawn surrounded by flower beds where roses seem to be throbbing with blood. Physical existence is so intensely present it is almost an oppression in the air. A stillness that chokes. And some of us cannot bear this reality, even the whispering leaves of the eucalyptus seem to be intent on crushing us with their weight, and we look up at the sky, at the fierce golden light edging a dark cloud and believe that we could, if only once in a lifetime, see a vision there, perhaps a chariot being drawn across the sky even though we are well aware that what we are likely to see is the next plane making its landing approach to the city.

There is a menace in things: a marble floor, a hairy wrist, is an inexplicable threat. Solid masses shudder. And yet in the uncertainty of our passions, things are what we must hold on to—the sapphire in the hand, the surfaces of furniture, or a memory of a furry animal. The mind seeks a purer thought, the soul an ecstasy, but the body, finding itself in a world of bourgeois objects, whether in Cheltenham or the suburbs of Sydney, is always a clumsy hindrance, and it must learn to accept the humiliation of having to crawl naked on all fours. The self, with all its attendant vanities, must be discarded on some shore before the weak flesh can enter the interior and the body be subjected to such savage humiliation that the soul finally has its chance to experience ecstasy. Though that, too, will be denied and existence will be reduced to meaningless pain.

The stripping of Ellen Roxburgh in *A Fringe of Leaves* by the savage women is a central symbol in the novels of Patrick White. Coming in one of his later novels, it is a moment towards which several of his earlier characters (Theodora Goodman, Laura Trevelyan, Voss, Miss Hare, Mordecai Himmelfarb) have been progressing, so to speak: each one is stripped metaphorically, and, given the obsessively repetitive nature of White's themes, it was almost inevitable that the veils of metaphor be finally torn away and the body be reduced to its bare, vulnerable flesh:

> If she sustained physical wounds from swooping branches, and half-rotted stumps or broken roots concealed in the humus underfoot, she neither whinged nor limped: the self which had withdrawn was scarcely conscious of them.

There is in Patrick White's characters a terrible desire to witness truth in one comprehensive vision; they are constantly turning their gaze towards the interior as if to enter some timeless zone of space would stifle the self and the soul thus freed would at last be in a state of readiness to receive the vision.

Strikingly—because the two novelists treat of such different surfaces—there is a parallel between White's characters and Beckett's: Mrs Hunter, lying in bed with nothing to wait for but death, is a Molloy or a Malone, enjoying or suffering the luxury or the pain of memories. Miss Hare sucks stones like Molloy (though, of course, no one does that exactly *like* Molloy!); Mrs Roxburgh and Jack Chance are Pim and Bom, journeying if not entirely through a sea of mud at least through a landscape familiar to Browning's Childe Roland and Shakespeare's Edgar; and Edgar, indeed, is the archetypal man who, together with Pim, Bom, Jack Chance and Mrs Roxburgh, might have been discovered by Lévi-Strauss in Amazonia as the nucleus of a tribe constituting a complete fundamental structure of human society. Both novelists use similarly desolate and hostile landscapes: White to sustain a spiritual, and Beckett a philosophical, tension. White draws upon the desert of Australia, and Beckett turns the world into a harsh abstraction of mud (the difference is as narrow and as great, depending on how one looks at the work, as between the desert painted by Georgia O'Keeffe and the late abstractions of Mark Rothko).

The difference between Beckett and White is one of literary convention, of form, and the intelligence of each is informed by a different philosophy; but the thrust of the imagination of each seems to be the same. Beckett's Watt at least can walk, after his own fashion, wear his bowler hat and great coat, but with Malone the body has become horizontal and useless, and by the time we get to Pim, the body is only an abstract idea. White's characters proceed tow\rds a similar state of non-being, but with this crucial difference: they continue to belong to that species of animal which needs to eat and defecate. But this difference comes from the convention of the traditional novel in which White works; his world is obliged to delineate the features of common reality, while Beckett, creating his own forms, can create his own world. Once we go beyond the variation of imagery that comes from the nature of the form in which each writer is working—in other words, once we grant each writer the language he has chosen—we then discover the congruent points where the two imaginations discover the same stark truth. It is hopeless; the vision we are after will not come. To have reverted, albeit involuntarily, to the condition of a primitive being, as has been Mrs Roxburgh's fate, has been only to discover that the body will suffer any indignity, including that of eating human flesh, in order to survive; the instinct to *be* is all; but if we had hoped for any revelation, in the extremity of our suffering the mind had had no existence and what there had been of soul had withdrawn. There is nothing to do but accept the empty world of tea-parties in Cheltenham. Beckett's characters, having long been absolved from life as we know it, cannot return but must continue crawling through the sea of mud, and meaninglessness must prevail.

The nature of what the imagination discovers is a

function of the language and the form in which the fiction is being created and its final shape is a characteristic of the style which the writer has attempted to perfect. Patrick White's novels, from early to the most recent, are bounded by the limitations of the traditional novel. His method is so stereotyped as to be embarrassing at times. He creates a gallery of characters, the lesser ones among whom are types we recognize as belonging to the nineteenth-century novel. In short, his entire approach is repugnant to twentieth-century sensibility. However, it would be an error to think that there is something *implicitly* right or wrong about any form; it is just that the post-Joycean reader has developed a snobbish preference and is conditioned to be more sympathetic to what proclaims itself as the new. The only question in fiction is: how good is this language? A novelist's success, and his failure, is always to be observed in his prose style. Two of White's novels, *A Fringe of Leaves* and *Riders in the Chariot*, exemplify how a writer, using the same traditional form for each, fails with one and creates a masterpiece in the other.

In the opening chapter of *A Fringe of Leaves*, three minor characters have just bid farewell to Ellen and Austin Roxburgh who have taken the *Bristol Maid* to England. The three discuss the Roxburghs and Garnet Roxburgh (the brother in Van Diemen's Land whom the Roxburghs had come to visit). The scene is a cliché from drawing-room comedies, and White, himself aware of the hackneyed nature of the device, ends the chapter with: 'The occupants of the carriage were rolled on into the deepening afternoon, and finally, like minor characters who have spoken a prologue, took themselves off into the wings.' It is a desperate attempt to win the connivance of the reader; and the remark by one of the characters on the same page—'I wonder,' he said, 'how Mrs Roxburgh would react to suffering if faced with it?'—is too transparent a statement of the novel's theme. After such a bald allusion, we can be pretty certain that Mrs Roxburgh will be faced with a great deal of suffering.

In the second chapter, predictably enough, the reader is offered portraits of Mr and Mrs Roxburgh. They are sitting in the saloon of the ship, and she is mending a shirt—a sort of theatre 'business' which has nothing to do with the action. The author first seats his model: 'Seated the other side of the table, her shawl fastened tighter against the draughts, she resumed her work of accommodating the shirt.' The author then draws the portrait:

> She was a woman of medium height, not above thirty years of age, which made her considerably younger than her husband. Without the cap she would have been wearing if discovered at home, the head looked rather larger than suited the proportions of her form, but presented without ornament or undue art, in the last of the winter afternoon, it had the unexpectedness of one of the less easily identified semi-precious stones in an unpretentious setting.

And so on for a paragraph of sixteen lines. It is a standard sort of description and is saved from being utterly hackneyed by White's prose. The last sentence in the above quotation, for example, is carefully crafted, has a lovely cadence (the positioning of the phrase 'in the last of the winter afternoon' and the poetical quality of the phrase itself are vital to the rhythm), and is made up of phrases in each of which something interesting is shown. However good the craft and lovely the prose, the portrait is nevertheless old-fashioned, and when it is finished, the author needs to bring the character back to active life. So the next paragraph begins with, 'Mrs Roxburgh laid aside the mending,' and the transitional moment allows the author to insert a fact: 'A lonely childhood, followed by marriage with a man twenty years her senior, had inclined her mind to reverie.' And, sure enough, a paragraph later we are in the middle of a flash-back, that easiest of novelistic devices.

Technically, a novelist could not be more crude than this, failing in his duty to keep his technique invisible. Chapter 3 does not improve matters, being built upon a series of flash-backs that take the reader back to Ellen Roxburgh's childhood in Cornwall, describe her marriage to Austin Roxburgh, bring the two to Van Diemen's Land to visit Garnet Roxburgh, and so on. While the technique is appalling, the matter, however, is interesting, and one recognizes it as belonging typically to White's imagination. While again and again, in all his novels, he descends to the most hackneyed level of structure, the strength of his prose allows him to sail sublimely across the shallowest approach. There is always something *interesting* in the shape of his sentences. What we learn of Ellen Roxburgh's past is familiar White territory. Her father was a drunk, and she the strong girl who 'drove him home from Penzance when drunk on market day'. It is she who struggles to keep the farm going, being, at this stage, the lowly, uneducated White character (like Stan Parker in *The Tree of Man*) whom life obliges to be heroic. She has, then, lived on the edge of suffering, or at least has experienced the anguish of coping with the father's incompetent body, unconsciously learning something about the body's failures. By the time she marries the frail, moralizing, and intellectually shallow Mr Roxburgh, she is already in the alien world where she can only expect a succession of trials.

White's principal characters do not enjoy the ordinary pleasures of nationality, matrimony, friendship, or any of the normal allegiances with which human beings codify the games calculated to relieve the anxiety about reality. Himmelfarb, in *Riders in the Chariot*, is driven out of his native Germany because he is a Jew; but he finds himself an outsider in Israel, too, and even when he is finally at home in Australia his alien condition is guaranteed by every gesture he makes and every word he utters. In Israel, he could have enjoyed the superficial fulfilment which he observes in his brother-in-law's life, but Australia offers the potential for suffering, that final mutation of the body which surely must, if only for a second, offer the comprehensive vision. And Voss, too, another German, leaving the lush forests and coming to Australia, seeks the most alien landscape of all, the desert, that interior which is almost a projection of the human soul, that final condition of alienation. White's Australia is often a desert even when he is describing life in the pretentious suburbs with their lawns and flower beds. Ellen Roxburgh is destined for the same pilgrimage, though her first move from the nearly barren farm in Cornwall is to the sterile world of Cheltenham. Much of this is overstated in Chapter 3; for example, the three paragraphs describing the wedding are quite unnecessary. The third paragraph reads:

> Aunt Tite, whose charity was only ever skin-deep, showed her generosity by choosing white satin and lace, with satin slippers and kid gloves, for her pauper niece. Hepzibah Tregaskis, as bridesmaid, wore rosebud pink which went with her pretty complexion. The bride, who had spent too much time in the fields, looked the swarthier for her white.

Compare this scene with the account of Himmelfarb's wedding in *Riders in the Chariot* where the wedding is described in terms of ritual and ceremony and the event captures the history of the race by sensitively transmitting a few key symbols in a richly evocative language, and one can comprehend the difference between writing which is merely filling the pages before the crucial action and writing which uses each event in its narrative to explore yet another dimension of the complexity of ideas available to the novelist.

Chapter 3 of *A Fringe of Leaves* contains, too, the kind of coincidence which is unthinkable in modern fiction: when Mrs Roxburgh goes riding on her brother-in-law Garnet's estate on Van Diemen's Land and is, as the reader had anticipated, thrown off the horse, Garnet comes along and proceeds to seduce her. This event is cheap enough to belong to the world of the popular novelist, but apparently at the very moment that she is being seduced by her brother-in-law, back at the house her husband Austin has an attack, as if his body must also suffer a form of violating penetration. However necessary the author might consider this coincidental action, it is nevertheless cheap melodrama. This is not a unique coincidence in White. In the same chapter, when the Roxburghs have left brother Garnet and are living in Hobart Town, Ellen, on a lonely walk, is pursued by a degenerate and is in danger of being rudely molested if not raped, when miraculously Garnet appears. And in *Voss*, to give one more example of this sort of melodramatic coincidence pervading so much of White's work, Laura Trevelyan in Sydney suffers a brain fever while Voss is experiencing physical mutilation in the desert. The symbolic intention behind such coincidences tends to scream a little too loudly at the reader.

If I dwell upon these failures of technique and handling of subject matter, it is to express a double astonishment: first, that in spite of the clichéd techniques and patently old-fashioned organization of his subject matter, White succeeds in creating an important body of fiction which is as compelling as that of his great contemporary Beckett; second, that a writer of such obvious genius should have so restricted himself that his attention to form is attention only to a formula. He does not win the reader with his form but with his thought, and his principal attraction to writers is the quality of his prose which even in one of his poorer novels, like *The Tree of Man*, is never without interest, and his style which is often dazzling. Many of his readers, however, unfortunately see the formal failure first and are led to abandon the work, and to them it is hard not to concede that the writer who has not been able to nourish the form of his art has, in the end, lost a serious audience (as has happened, or must inevitably happen, with Arnold Bennett, E. M. Forster, Steinbeck and Hemingway). When one pays more attention to a novel's subject matter than to its style, it is a sure sign that the work in question is of an inferior sort. No novelist can escape Flaubert's axiom, 'that there is no such thing as subject, style in itself being an absolute manner of seeing things.'

Chapter 3 of *A Fringe of Leaves* contains another hackneyed device: quotations from the characters' journals. After recording the resumption of the voyage, Mr Roxburgh writes:

> From the little we have seen of this Colony after the comparatively fertile expanses of Van Diemen's Land, there was never an emptier, more hostile country (E. not altogether in agreement because of the fanciful, or 'romantic', streak in her nature).

Here are two images that infuse much of White's fiction: the empty, hostile country and the character with the 'romantic' streak in her nature. If Mr Roxburgh excludes himself from being a romantic, it is because his insistence on rational control is so deliberate that he does not perceive his self-consciously orthodox rationality to be, in itself, a form of romanticism. He is helpless and incompetent, demands a fussy attentiveness, and yet attempts to project an image of himself as one who can offer a salvation of sorts to his wife, little knowing that it is he himself who is the *burnt one* (to use a phrase which is the title of one of White's volumes of short stories: his characters often are *the burnt ones*). His journal records the anguish of one major type of White character: to want a serenity of soul but to suffer always from some doubt, to long for visions and to perceive only shadows. It is a profound and an inexplicable sense of suffering, and the character, a Christian, can find no language in which to define his anguish.

Mrs Roxburgh's journal presents a second major type of White character who is seen as an antithesis of the first: the nearly pagan person who experiences an ecstasy which must remain her secret, for she cannot communicate it, especially not to the uncomprehending soul of a solemn Christian like her husband. Her journal attests to experiences of dizziness similar to that of many of White's major characters; they should have been artists, but bourgeois society with its Christian lip service has prevented that. Alf Dubbo in *Riders to the Chariot* pours out his vision onto canvas and, revealingly, he is an aborigine, as savage a mind as any Lévi-Strauss might have found, and intuitively he is as precise in capturing the structure of the vision as any civilized character might have been. Where Dubbo is saved from the interior by the well-meaning Christians and made a free individual in a civilized society, Mrs Roxburgh is driven into the interior by circumstances and becomes a slave in an aboriginal society. Taking to drink and not understanding his own imagination, Dubbo arrives at Christian myth in his paintings, while Mrs Roxburgh is deprived of any further spiritual drunkenness and can think only of basic survival, as any savage is obliged to, becoming briefly a cannibal.

The rest of Chapter 3 contains flash-backs mainly of the visit to Garnet Roxburgh. Chapter 4 resumes the voyage on the *Bristol Maid* and contains information about Austin Roxburgh, again presented in flash-backs. One significant statement occurs in this chapter: Ellen Roxburgh thinks, in a dream, 'I will, I *must* endure it because this is my only purpose.'—which could be the theme of the book. A rather trite symbolic image appears at the end of the chapter: Mr Roxburgh has had another attack; she fetches him some milk and presently he falls asleep; she lies next to him, 'his cheek fretting against one of her breasts. The breast had escaped from its covering, at its centre the teat on which his struggling mouth once or twice threatened to fasten.'

In Chapter 5 the ship strikes a reef, and Mrs Roxburgh reveals to her husband that she is pregnant. Together with the crew, they take to the boats, and Chapter 6 describes the usual struggles of the shipwrecked. A boy named Oswald Dignam, who for some reason had thought of Mrs Roxburgh as a 'Divine Presence', drowns while attempting to get her some shellfish. She delivers a stillborn child. Another member of the crew dies and is pitched overboard without ceremony.

I give these bare details in order to indicate that they are like those in any old shipwreck story, for what dramatic action there is in these chapters is predictable. Admittedly, White's prose is rarely without interest, and one does perceive his intention of wanting to submit a diverse group of people to the severest trial to see what will be left of their humanity and to confirm to himself again the spiritual frailty of mankind as well as the meaninglessness of human ideas in an elemental and hostile universe. But we saw all this as long ago as *Voss*, and the oceanic struggle in the later book is only a replay of Voss's and his companions' struggle in the desert. There is nothing in the ideas relating to the group which the White reader does not already know by heart. It is all unnecessary, and parts of these chapters read like a schoolboy's adventure story—for example, the land they first sight turns out to be only a reef. It is surprising to see White, so late in his career, expend so much labour merely to fulfil the conventional demands of his form. It is as if Beckett, when he came to write *How It Is*, took two hundred pages to tell us how the narrator first fell out of a tram like Watt, then cycled across the country like Molloy, and finally entered the sea of mud. Reduce *A Fringe of Leaves* to Chapter 7, and you have as magnificent a novel as the modern imagination has conceived. Instead, the first six chapters with their predictable plot, together with the eighth chapter in which Mrs Roxburgh is safely back in the world she had left, an ending which would have satisfied Flannery O'Connor's aunt who could not be content with a fiction unless there was a happy resolution which rounded it off, make *A Fringe of Leaves* little more than a survival story.

Chapter 7 could easily have degenerated to the sort of anthropological pretentiousness one sees in Golding's *Lord of the Flies*; instead, White, while obviously drawing upon anthropological data, focuses entirely upon the natural barbarity of the human body in order to commit the body to that degree of violent suffering in which the mind will cast the self aside and thus be prepared to receive the comprehensive vision. In this chapter, White is pursuing truth and not merely filling out his story with the dramatic episodes necessary to it. It is a beautiful and perfectly complete narrative. It is the primal novel with its ancient theme of endurance. The chapter begins:

> All trace of cloud was gone from the sky as they approached the shore. Faces bleared by rain and suffering offered themselves instead to an onslaught by ceremonial sunlight, which was grinding an already dazzling stretch of sand into an ever-intensifying white. Some of the castaways would not have been surprised had the Almighty ordered His trumpets to sound their arrival on the fringe of paradise itself.

The first two sentences have the immediacy of good descriptive writing, plunging the reader into crucial action, and at the same time suggest White's ironical perception which, in the third sentence, is reinforced by 'the fringe of paradise'. This is the *place*, then, to which the voyagers have been destined to come attended by 'cere-monial sunlight' which, however, far from promising a continuing benevolence, will turn this kind clarity to a blinding abstract whiteness. They are no longer voyagers, though; only 'castaways', thrown out by the ocean, given a momentary birth and the passing illusion of God's presence and His personal attention to their salvation, and the land they have come to is the primeval earth which has the deceptive appearance of a 'fringe of paradise'.

Tumbling out of the longboat, most of the survivors 'crawl like maimed crabs through the shallows' to come to the paradise which first offers their famished appetites the stinking and putrefying carcass of a kangaroo and their thirst pools of brackish water, a combination that gives most of them diarrhoea. At night, when they have camped, 'Mrs Roxburgh would have given thanks . . . had it not been for a curious noise, of animal gibbering, or human chatter, slight at first, then sawing louder into the silence.' The thought of prayer is neatly extinguished by the presence of savages, and the human voice which can utter so much sweet reason and be so melodious in expressing praise of the Lord is now heard as 'animal gibbering'. Language is replaced by noise, salvation by an unthought-of horror. God has failed once again, His paradise has receded, or perhaps He intends only a succession of horrors to visit his creatures; and it is not long before the entire party, except for Ellen Roxburgh, is either murdered or taken away by the savages. When the dying Mr Roxburgh calls to his wife to pray for him, 'She could not, would never pray again. "Oh, no, Lord! Why are we born, then?" ' There is no answer. She sees flies 'crowding in black dots' around her husband's mouth.

The savage women come for Mrs Roxburgh and begin by flinging sand in her face. The two pages describing her humiliation and stripping at the hands of the 'monkey-women' evoke horror, disgust, and pity, and it is at this point, now that Mrs Roxburgh is left naked and makes for herself 'a fringe of leaves' to wind around her waist, that the novel's true substance begins to be presented. This is when her 'self' withdraws. From this moment until her re-entry into the 'civilized' world, she will have only her body.

This body is at once reduced to a condition lower than that of a dog; for she thinks in her hunger, 'Could she perhaps crawl out after dark and scavenge for the bones of those small furred animals? But dogs carried off any remains their masters had failed to swallow. One partially bald cur bit her as she tried to seduce him into sharing his booty.' And this body must suffer a hideous transformation: 'Three of them seized her by the hair, stretching it to full length, even yanking at it for extra measure, while one beefier female began hacking at the roots with a shell.' So that she finds herself 'become a stubbled fright such as those around her, or even worse':

> But the women had not finished their work. They dragged her to her feet. Next the hide of some animal was brought, filled with a rancid fat with which they smeared their passive slave; she could but submit to her anointing, followed by an application of charcoal rubbed with evident disgust, if not spite, into the shamefully white skin.

Nor is this suffering enough; for White, seeking that image which must turn the stomach of his reader with a vivid evocation of disgust, makes the savage women oblige Mrs Roxburgh to carry a sick child: 'She looked down once and saw the pus from her charge's sores uniting with the sweat on her own charcoal-dusted arms.' The reader experiences the disgust more revoltingly than Mrs Roxburgh, for her mind is upon the 'delicious smell of dew rising from the grass' and upon the blue sky—pastoral images of happiness. Where her condition has been reduced to her body melting with the diseases of her burden and existence to the image of pus flowing upon her flesh, she can think only of survival: 'But she would not, must not die—why, she could not imagine'. And yet she stifles her mind's 'search for a cause or reason for her presence in a clueless maze.' The intellect will not help her, a conviction shared by several of White's characters.

She must see, too, what has become of the bodies of the other castaways:

> Amongst charred branches and the white flock of ash gone cold, lay a man's body set in a final anguished curve, the roasted skin noticeably crackled down one side from shoulder to thigh. One of the legs had been hacked away from where the thigh is joined to the hip. If the skull, bared to the bone in places by wilful gashes, grimaced at the intruder through singed whisker and a crust of blood, grime, and burning, the mouth atoned for all that is fiendish by its resignation to suffering.

What can such unceremonious dismemberment of the body mean but that Mrs Roxburgh is made to witness the collapse of her husband's faith and reason. Even his constant companion Virgil did not take him anywhere but to a horrible death, and here is the roasted and mutilated body of the first officer whose seamanship has not helped him on his journey. The desperate anguish of White's characters from Eden Standish, in *The Living and the Dead*, to the Princess de Lascabanes, in *The Eye of the Storm*, is here put to the extremest test. There is no question here of moral failure or is there, in an awfully empty world, any alternative of hope and fulfilment somehow asserting itself; for the entire language of civilization no longer exists in the dark world surrounding Mrs Roxburgh. She does not see Christian death, only a body one of whose limbs has provided food for the primitive human tribe. White, who had in *Riders in the Chariot* submitted a human being to a crucifixion and observed that even in that extremity there had been no vision, but only a *reflection* of God, inevitably had to arrive at this chapter in which the body's suffering is of the worst imaginable type: the crucified Himmelfarb could at least aspire to spiritual ecstasy in the midst of his pain and derive some sense of triumph from the knowledge that the people crucifying him, though barbarians, were Christians who knew the symbolism of their action and would later repent, but there is no redemption in being mutilated by cannibalistic savages. And even this final catastrophe of the body offers nothing but a hopeless despair. No, nothing helps, there is no salvation, there are no visions; the body will submit itself to any horror in order to survive.

And Mrs Roxburgh survives, with the help of Jack Chance (a name so obviously a reflection on the accident of his opportune coming that it has to be deliberate, as if White were determined to show that Mrs Roxburgh's survival, being entirely due to chance, did not necessarily imply the triumph of the pagan over the Christian). Their escape from the primitive tribe, their struggle together through the hostile territory, and their love-making, which is nearly as absurd as in Beckett's novels, are all touched by a sort of resigned desperation.

This has to be, this cannot be; this should not be but is; this is existence, survival. This toothless mouth attempting a kiss and being eagerly accepted; this withering breast whose wrinkles are veins throbbing with passion. Ah, life!

The body was not so important in *Riders in the Chariot* in which the main characters are at least plain or physically ungainly, if not downright ugly. Of all White's novels, *Riders in the Chariot* and *The Eye of the Storm* are the most perfectly realized: they are his masterpieces; indeed, they are masterpieces by any standard. (I must add, in answer to the raised eyebrows of those of my contemporaries who dogmatically maintain that anyone working in the conventional novel cannot be taken seriously, that there is nothing more boring than the *programme* of the avant-garde with its self-congratulatory exclusiveness, that the only test, as Henry James said, is the test of execution. In *Riders in the Chariot* and *The Eye of the Storm*, White is as good as Beckett in his trilogy, and in the former book he has written a novel which has the poetic intensity of Eliot's *The Waste Land*.)

The religious symbolism of *Riders in the Chariot*, in which Himmelfarb, the Jew, is crucified and dies on a Good Friday, will be comprehended by most readers and needs no explanation. But the book is not so much about religion as about religious experience, or, more precisely, vision—that capacity of the soul to be witness of an incommunicable sensation, or, in the words of the epigraph from Blake, to have discovered 'the infinite in everything'. During the crucifixion,

> Himmelfarb had known that he possessed the strength, but did pray for some sign. Through all the cursing, and trampling, and laughter, and hoisting, and aching, and distortion, he had continued to expect. Until now, possibly, it would be given. So, he raised his head. And was conscious of a stillness and clarity, which was the stillness and clarity of pure water, at the centre of which his God was reflected.

That is his moment of vision. Miss Hare, who watches over his dying, feels 'that she was being dispersed, but that in so experiencing, she was entering the final ecstasy.' And Alf Dubbo, painting what he had at last seen, 'smiled at his vision of the Mother of God waiting to clothe the dead Christ in white, and almost at once went into another part of the room, where he stood trembling and sweating. He thought he might not be able to continue.'

In an eloquent, though silent, scene, Dubbo, a naturally gifted painter, is led by some invisible force of destiny to stand outside a shed and witness the dying Jew being cared for by the two Marys (Mrs Godbold and Miss Hare) and a young man, with several of Mrs Godbold's children present:

> So, in his mind, he loaded with panegyric blue the tree from which the women and the young man His disciple, were lowering their Lord. And the flowers of the tree lay at its roots in pools of deepening blue. And the blue was reflected in the skins of the women and the young girl. As they lowered their Lord with that almost breathless love, the first Mary received him with her whitest linen, and the second Mary, who had appointed herself the guardian of his feet, kissed the bones which were showing through the cold, yellow skin.

This is the one scene in the novel when the four characters come together as participants and witnesses in an awesome ceremony of 'the supreme act of love'; there is no speech, and the intensity of emotion is all the more powerful for not being mentioned at all. (Similarly, later when Dubbo is at work: 'Much was omitted, which, in its absence, conveyed.') Simple details, all to do with common human actions, accumulate into a content of emotion, and by presenting the scene from the painter's point of view and dwelling upon visual details of colour and form, squeezing his words out of tubes, as it were, White gives the reader the same experience he might have standing in front of an Italian fresco. Consciously and with an acute sense of awareness, Dubbo witnesses the very images of the painting which had been in his imagination for years, revealing glimpses of itself from time to time but never appearing to him as the one comprehensive vision. Now he sees it in reality. When he begins to paint, the proportions of his picture 'suddenly appeared so convincing, so unshakeably right, they might have existed many years in his mind.' After he has painted

Christ, 'he ventured to retouch the wounds of the dead Christ with the love that he had never dared express in life, and at once the blood was gushing from his own mouth, the wounds in the canvas were shining and palpitating with his own conviction.' Dubbo is dying of tuberculosis, and the gushing of his own blood across the canvas is an awfully precise metaphor for the artist giving his life to his work. Finishing the painting, Dubbo keeps his vision, and he is compelled to paint *'the Chariot-thing'* which has haunted him all his life. He dies soon after, having exhausted his body in pouring out his visions.

Two ironies attend his death: it is Dubbo, who has perceived that illusion is also truth, who both captures and is killed by the intensity of his visions; he, the savage, is possessed by religious ecstasy while the nearest his original guardian, the Rev. Timothy Calderon, had come to any ecstasy at all was when he committed a homosexual act upon the boy Dubbo. There is the suggestion that public religion offers no salvation, that it is ugly and vulgar, for the truly religious people in the book are Dubbo, Miss Hare and Mrs Godbold, each of them informed in their spiritual quest by intimations of the soul and not by an institutionalized faith. The second irony is that the paintings which contain Dubbo's visions perform no revolutionary function in society; the landlady who discovers them after Dubbo's death sells them at an auction 'where they fetched a few shillings, and caused a certain ribaldry.' After that, 'the paintings disappeared, and, if not destroyed when they ceased to give the buyers a laugh, have still to be discovered'. The artist's vision remains his own: we may be moved or provoked into hilarity by a picture, but we never see what the artist saw, we never witness another's truth.

The scene in which the death of Christ occurs both in the reality of Himmelfarb's life as well as in the imagination of Dubbo, the artist, takes place some sixty pages from the end of the novel and is preceded by nearly five hundred pages of an intricate plot. It is astonishing that the technical devices in this novel are not transparent. White needs to give the complete histories of his main characters which, in the Himmelfarb section, involve going back to pre-Nazi Germany and creating the world of German Jews, and the obvious device is the flash-back. White disposes of transitions and simply plunges into blocks of time and experience, making each event an immediate sensation by creating a prose which is rich in capturing the textures of surfaces and the depths of feelings, so that the reader, absorbed on each page in immediate time and experience, is not conscious of the technique.

The first chapter of some ten pages is broken into five sections so that the past and the present are deliberately and conspicuously made to alternate. The second section begins, 'In the past . . .'; the fourth with the words, 'Once or twice in the far past . . .'; and the fifth with, 'And now . . .' In this short chapter, by relating a few images from the past while maintaining the present focus, White establishes a conviction in the reader's mind that the past and the present have a simultaneous existence, so that, when in later chapters he needs to present a longer narrative from the past, the reader's mind has been conditioned to receive that, too, as immediate experience.

The novel begins with a portrait of Mary Hare who lives alone in a fabulous mansion called Xanadu which, however, has begun to decay. She is shown to be eccentric and somewhat comical at first—'part woman, part umbrella'; the concluding words of the first paragraph about her are calculated both to be amusing as well as to convey an impression of an extraordinary creature. She is seen to be wearing an old hat 'which she wore summer and winter regardless, and which gave her at times the look of a sunflower, at others, just an old basket coming to pieces.' A misfit in the world of human time, she has no sense of things, prefers animals, birds and plants to people, and is herself, 'like any wild thing native to the place', a creature of instincts who crawls through the undergrowth finding the leaf mould 'lovely if the knees were allowed to sink for a moment'. She is ugly, 'a small, freckled thing', and 'when she spoke, her mouth stayed stiff, almost as if she had had a stroke'. She is inept with language: 'abstractions made her shiver.' The portrait is built over several pages, and what is created is one of White's most perfectly realized characters, a human being who has no commerce with society, who finds the material world incomprehensible, and yet who has been led 'to expect of life some ultimate revelation'. Somehow she has been chosen to suffer, as also have been Mrs Godbold, Himmelfarb and Dubbo.

White goes back to the childhood of each character and produces a complete history in such brilliant detail that each one could be a perfectly beautiful novel in itself except for White's larger purpose of showing how destiny brings these four people, scattered in different parts of the earth, together in one moment of suffering which is so intense that it has the dazzling whiteness of the vision each one has been seeking; of showing, too, a world populated by dead souls, living in different stages of petrifaction in deserts of suburbia or in cellular hovels of the modern city.

The most memorable, and also the most painful, of the four histories is that of Himmelfarb, born in a Jewish family in Germany. He is an exceptionally talented scholar, masters several languages as a boy, becomes a professor, and would have had a distinguished career but for the Nazis; when he comes to Australia he says quietly, 'The intellect has failed us'. After this statement, he speaks very little, seeming to abandon language as a medium of discovery, and works at jobs, like cleaning public lavatories, that are almost a calculated insult to the intellect.

Earlier in his life in Germany, 'spiritually he longed for the ascent into an ecstasy so cool and green that his own desert would drink the heavenly moisture'; and 'he was racked by his persistent longing to exceed the bounds of reason: to gather up the sparks, visible intermittently inside the thick shells of human faces; to break through the sparks of light imprisoned in the forms of wood and stone'. But experience intervenes and mocks the pretensions of the intellect that it can arrive at knowledge. He must suffer. But though his house and his family are destroyed and though he, too, finds himself on a train packed with Jews being taken to a concentration camp, he remains the chosen one: his suffering is going to be that he will survive and cross to another desert with an ever-present memory of past pain and come to a death more cruel and brutal than even one in the gas chamber.

White's narrative of Himmelfarb's journey is presented with horrifying vividness. There is, among other Jews on the train, the Lady from Czernowitz who talks gaily and optimistically. While the reader is kept aware of the other people on the train and is anxious about Himmelfarb's fate, the Lady from Czernowitz becomes the point of focus. Hers is a life of common hopes and the innocent ambition to live in social splendour; she is boastful, opinionated, self-deceiving, pretentious, and convinced that she has the highest taste; in short, she is an ordinary human being. And when the final horror comes, it is presented through her:

> She stood there for an instant in the doorway, and might have fallen if allowed to remain longer. Her scalp was grey stubble where the reddish hair had been. Her one dug hung down beside the ancient scar which represented the second. Her belly sloped away from the hillock of her navel. Her thighs were particularly poor. But it was her voice which lingered. Stripped. Calling to him from out of the dark of history, ageless, and interminable.

Calling to him. The scene at the concentration camp

dissolves with that voice ringing in one's ears. The *voice*: the entire episode has been built around the idea of the voice. Before the Jews are put on the train 'the voices of all' are heard in prayer. The Lady from Czernowitz's voice has been professionally trained. ' "Welcome! Welcome!" announced the official voice, magnified' when they arrive at the camp. The voice becomes a scream when the Lady from Czernowitz realizes what is about to happen—' "I cannot bear it!" she shrieked. "I cannot bear it! Oh, no! No! No! No!" '; and when someone comforts her with the offer of prayers, 'Nor did she hear the man's voice attempting to grapple with a situation which might have tested the prophets themselves'; after she is taken away, ' "*Achtung! Achtung!* " the official voice prepared to inform.' Himmelfarb whispers, 'Into your hands, O Lord,' and finally that interminable voice 'Calling to him from out of the dark of history . . .'.

Himmelfarb carries that voice within him but is impatient of human discourse. On the journey to Israel, 'he was reluctant to lift up his voice with those of his fellow passengers' and does not respond when the younger passengers 'called to him, inviting him to participate in their relief and joy'. How could he who had been helpless when the Lady from Czernowitz had called to him? And what relief and joy can there be for a soul which has witnessed the triumph of evil? Israel itself depresses him with its self-congratulatory ardour, and his dialogue with his brother-in-law Ari in the *kibbutz* articulates his rejection of the new Zionist enthusiasm and also perhaps of the chosen land. He tells Ari:

Nothing, alas, is permanent. Not even this valley. Not even our Land. The earth is in revolt. It will throw up fresh stones—tonight—tomorrow—always. And you, the chosen, will continue to need your scapegoat, just as some of us do not wait to be dragged out, but continue to offer ourselves.

It is the last 'intellectual' statement he makes before going on to Australia.

There he is crucified and nearly attains that beatific vision which his soul hungers for, seeing his God reflected in an illusion of clear water in the extremity of his pain during the crucifixion. After he has been taken down from the tree, Mrs Godbold has him brought to her shed. And there 'He was swallowed up by the whiteness. He was received, as seldom. . . . Again, he was the Man Kadmon, descending from the Tree of Light to take the Bride. . . . As he received her, she bent and kissed the wound in his hand. Then they were truly one.' And there he dies, attended by the two Marys and watched from a window by Alf Dubbo.

Mrs Godbold endures while Dubbo, too, dies and Miss Hare simply disappears. Mrs Godbold is the earth mother and is rarely without a child at her breast and another in her belly. She is patient, silent, benevolent, washing laundry day after day. Coming from the grey land of the fens in England, she, too, is in the human desert, but her shed is surrounded by wild-flowering bushes, and her girls go about wearing garlands of 'any old common flowers'. She meekly accepts punishment and hardship: once when her daughter Gracie comes running in and announces 'I am saved for Jesus!' Tom Godbold, the drunken father, begins to beat his wife. 'Mrs Godbold bent her head. Her eyelids flickered. There was such a beating and fluttering of light, and white wings. She was, all in all, dazed.' She does not understand abstract words but has knowledge within her: 'Finally the woman sitting alone in the deserted shed would sense how she had shot her six arrows at the face of darkness, and halted it.' What is more, 'she herself was, in fact, the infinite quiver.' And the last words of the novel are: 'she continued to live.' She, too, is touched by light:

That evening, as she walked along the road, it was the

hour at which the other gold sank its furrows in the softer sky. The lids of her eyes, flickering beneath its glow, were gilded with an identical splendour. But for all its weight, it lay lightly, lifted her, in fact, to where she remained an instant in the company of Living Creatures she had known, and many others she had not. All was ratified again by hands.

Images of light permeate the entire book, usually in relation to one of the four main characters, from 'an early pearliness of light' on the first page of the novel to 'the dazzle' in its last sentence. There are several other recurring images—the *house*, for one. Xanadu, a monument to Norbert Hare's vision of splendour, collapses, is razed to the dust together with its garden and surrounding park, and replaced by a cheap subdivision. Himmelfarb's house in Germany is invaded by Nazis, those agents of destruction more efficient than termites, and his hut in Sarsaparilla is burned down. There is Mrs Flack's house, ironically named 'Karma', which harbours her evil, and the Rosetrees' house, which is the bourgeoisie's idea of paradise on earth and where the Catholic Harry Rosetree is overwhelmed by his earlier identity, that of the Jew Haïm Rosenbaum, and hangs himself. Only Mrs Godbold's shed, harbouring no guilt or deception and receiving the dying Christ as an ordinary event, possesses a natural beauty, for out of it flows life.

There is the imagery of hell, suggested first in Nazi Germany and then used most deliberately in the closing chapter where Mrs Flack and Mrs Jolley are trapped in 'Karma':

> Night thoughts were cruellest, and often the two women, in their long, soft, trailing gowns, would bump against each other in the passages, or fingers encountered fingers, and they would lead each other gently back to the origins of darkness. They were desperately

necessary to each other in threading the labyrinth. Without proper guidance, a soul in hell might lose itself.

In the same chapter, Mrs Chalmers-Robinson, Mrs Wolfson, and Mrs Colquhon sit in a 'darkened restaurant', almost as if condemned to the place, 'craning in hopes that saving grace might just become visible in the depths of the obscure purgatory in which they sat'. The three rich women simply sit there, and 'each of the three tried to remember where she would go next'. And the new middle class living behind the 'wafer-walls of the new homes' is condemned to its hell, an endless, meaningless motion: 'All of Sunday they would visit, or be visited, though sometimes they would cross one another, midway, while remaining unaware of it. Then, on finding nothing at the end, they would drive around, or around. They would drive and look for something to look at. . . . So the owners of the new homes drove. They drove around.' They are in the inescapable circles of hell. These are also images of the wasteland in which people have lost direction and purpose. Suburban life is glimpsed from a train:

In the kitchens of many homes, gentlemen in singlets were only now assaulting their plastic sausages, ladies were limply tumbling the spaghetti off the toast on which they had been so careful to put it, daughters daintier than their mums were hurrying to get finished, for ever, but for ever. Over all, the genie of beef dripping still hovered in his blue robe. But magic was lacking. And in narrow rooms, emptied boys, rising from sticky contemplation of some old coloured pin-up, prepared to investigate the dark.

A vision of the city intensifies the imagery of the sick, squalid society:

The neon syrup coloured the pools of vomit and the sailors' piss. By that light, the eyes of the younger, gaberdine men were a blinding, blinder blue, when not actually burnt out. The blue-haired grannies had purpled from the roots of their hair down to the ankles of their pants, not from shame, but neon, as their breasts chafed to escape, from shammy-leather back to youth, or else roundly asserted themselves, like chamberpots in concrete.

Coming to the ocean offers no escape from the wasteland: 'The waters of Babylon had not sounded sadder than the sea, ending on a crumpled beach, in a scum of French-letters.' A song is heard on a radio—'O rivers of vomit, O little hills of concupiscence, O immense plains of complacency!'

The entire passage is a remarkable echo of *The Waste Land* right down to the technique of using a fragment of a song, to say nothing of the idea of the journey, or pilgrimage, and the imagery of water and sterile sexuality, and it is as effective in showing the desolation of the human spirit. And this world, a world inescapably that of the living dead, forms a background to the spiritual quest of the four main characters (of whom only Himmelfarb has been deliberately a seeker while the others simply find it in their nature to be separate from humanity). White's vision is bitterly pessimistic: while he can create in Himmelfarb the concept of greatness potentially accessible to the human spirit and in Dubbo the primeval rage of the artist, White is not a sentimentalist but merely a witness to the fact that lives such as these are exceptions in the modern desert. There is no rain-bearing thunder at the end of his epic; instead, Xanadu is 'shaved right down to a bald, red rudimentary hill', and mindless existence prevails. The human soul has been emptied of dreams and magic.

In his later years, Bento Santiago, the hero of Machado de Assis' *Dom Casmurro*, builds a house in a suburb of Rio de Janeiro where, exhausted by the monotony of working in the garden or reading, he decides to write a book in order to pass the time. He thinks of writing a *History of the Suburbs* but he is prompted instead to write about himself, for the 'act of narration would summon the illusion' of his existence. The house he has built is an exact copy of his parents' house, the scene of his earlier happiness, and although he inherited that house he allowed it to be torn down because it seemed to have become an alien place. In building a copy of the old house, Dom Casmurro has created a stage for the drama of his own life: he has removed himself from his reality and at the same time created a replica of that reality. The image of the theatre is carefully hinted at when he says of the living room: 'In the four corners of the ceiling, are the figures of the seasons; and in the centre of the walls, the medallions of Caesar, Augustus, Nero and Massinissa, with their names beneath.' For that is the kind of decoration to be seen in old theatres. The metaphor of the theatre appears in many other instances in the novel. The name Don Casmurro is a nick-name acquired by Bento in later life, it is a name given to a 'morose, tight-lipped' *character*, it is a mask which this player cannot remove. When he was young, Bento could not sometimes tell whether his beloved Capitú was being herself or only acting. Dom Casmurro occasionally goes to the theatre; he has seen *Othello* and recognized his own tormenting passion on the stage.

When Dom Casmurro begins his narrative, the first memory which comes to him is of an afternoon when he, as Bento, is already fifteen. 'Actually it was the beginning of my life; all that had gone before was like the making-up and putting on costume of those about to go on stage, like the turning up of the lights, the tuning of the fiddles, the overture. . . . Now I was to commence my opera.'

And thus the action begins on the stage and consists of a

series of episodes which originally happened in another arena, but one not unlike the present theatre. Bento lives with his widowed mother, Dona Gloria, and spends much of his time playing innocently with Capitú, the neighbour's fourteen year old daughter. On that afternoon with which the narrative opens, José Dias, a dependent of the household, reminds Dona Gloria of the promise she had made to God after losing her first son, that should He bless her with another she would raise him as a priest. The time has come to fulfil that promise: Bento is of age to enter the seminary and, José Dias informs the mother, it should be done immediately for there would be an enormous difficulty should the young boy fall in love with the neighbour's daughter. Bento, who overhears the dialogue, recognizes for the first time the nature of his attachment to Capitú and is simultaneously horrified by the idea of both an immediate separation from her by being sent to a seminary and also a permanent separation should he become a priest.

The solemn promise, as in a folk-tale or in classical drama, if it is kept, will lead to one tragedy, and if it is not, to some unforeseen evil, which will be another tragedy; the beauty of Machado's novel is that it is a comedy which cannot prevent a tragic outcome, for its hero has within him not a tragic flaw but a flawless passion. It is life and how it contaminates the beauty that we believe it to possess which is the agent of destruction; or, to put it in another way, it is a feeling of repugnance for what existence means that makes us reject life, as Dom Casmurro does.

After Bento and Capitú have exhanged the vow during their adolescence that they will never marry if they cannot marry each other. Bento enters the seminary where he makes the friendship of Escobar. Neither Bento nor Escobar wishes to be ordained and since Escobar is under no compulsion of a parental promise he turns to the field he loves best, commerce; after the discussion of a fine theological point, a way out is discovered for Bento: an orphan boy is found to substitute for him, for the Church agrees with a new interpretation of the mother's promise—she had only promised *a* priest to God and he need not be her own son.

About three-quarters of the novel is over by the time Bento takes his degree in law and marries Capitú. Escobar has married a girl called Sancha, and the four live happily in close proximity. Life could not be more perfect. Sancha gives birth to a daughter but Capitú remains childless, making her own and Bento's life sad. Finally, Capitú gives birth to a boy, who is named Ezekiel, after Escobar, just as Sancha's daughter has been named after Capitú. The happiness of the two families, during which time the parents have fond visions of their children growing up, falling in love and marrying each other to perpetuate the perfect harmony of the two families, is brief, however. As Ezekiel grows up, Bento notices that he looks more and more like Escobar; the doubt in his mind becomes a raging jealousy: Bento is convinced that Capitú has been unfaithful to him and that his best friend is the father of the child. The action now takes place very rapidly; one event quickly follows another, each being described with the greatest economy. Escobar drowns while swimming in a violent sea; Sancha goes to live with her parents in a remote state; Bento takes Capitú and Ezekiel to Switzerland to effect a symbolic divorce and leaves them there, never to see Capitú again. Ezekiel returns when he is a grown man by which time, in Bento's eyes, he looks exactly like Escobar. When Ezekiel, who is now an archaeologist, suggests that he would like to pursue his work in the Middle East, Bento is happy to see him go and gives him the money he needs. Ezekiel contracts typhoid fever in Palestine and dies. The mask of Dom Casmurro now covers the face of Bento.

Did the breaking of the solemn promise lead to this tragic outcome? Machado hints that Dom Casmurro is the victim of a pathological jealousy; and Casmurro himself is aware of freak resemblances among people, for many years earlier Sancha's father had shown him a portrait of his wife and had pointed out how alike her face was to Capitú's, saying, 'Sometimes, in life, there are these strange resemblances'. But there is more than the strange resemblance which might, or might not, have been accidental. Dom Casmurro, gripped by the rage of his jealousy and blind to all else, does not realize that he is jealous not of his friend Escobar as much as he is of his son, for his jealousy only emerges some time after Ezekiel has been born. When the son returns from Europe, Dom Casmurro observes: 'He was dressed in modern clothes, naturally, and his manners were different, but the general aspect reproduced him who was dead. He was the self-same, the identical, the true Escobar'. In those two sentences, he is noting only what he believes to be the case, that Ezekiel now resembles Escobar so much that he is identical with him. But these sentences are immediately followed by, 'He was my wife's lover; the son of his father.' Dom Casmurro does not himself understand what he has said in that sentence, but Machado surely must have done, for the sentence is too carefully constructed and too neatly placed to be merely the kind of paradoxical phrase inserted only for rhetorical effect. Escobar was never Capitú's lover; but as soon as Ezekiel was born, *he* was—at least in his father's eyes who has proceeded to reject the son by *making* him in the image of the only person who could possibly have been his wife's lover, Escobar. The fact is that no one else but Dom Casmurro sees Escobar and Ezekiel as being 'identical'.

By creating the fantasy that his wife has been unfaithful to him, Dom Casmurro can seek the separation from Capitú which his rational self would not have permitted. The all-consuming love to which his eyes were opened at the age of fifteen is over by the time the son is born. And just before he begins to imagine the affair between Capitú and Escobar, Bento himself experiences a moment of lust for Sancha, and in that moment he is aware that Sancha's eyes have 'something quite different' in them from 'fraternal expansiveness'. This flickering of lust within himself, with its associated guilt, contributes to his imagining that the other pair, Escobar and Capitú, are guilty in fact. In this sense, he is jealous not because his wife has been unfaithful but because of his realization that he himself has the potential for infidelity, a suppressed thought that tears at his conception of the perfect and innocent love of his adolescence. If he and Sancha can experience a moment of lust for each other, can it not be that Escobar and Capitú have shared the same experience, from which it must follow that perhaps they have already carried that feeling beyond the realm of fantasy.

Dom Casmurro's tragedy is that time exists. The rejected son has been the most vivid reminder of time. Reality has been made unbearable, and Dom Casmurro can only see himself as a tragic figure in some fiction, an Othello, trapped within a theatre where he must continually re-enact the years of his adolescence which had seemed timeless, but with a knowledge of the tragedy which follows those enchanting years.

Dom Casmurro was written at the end of the nineteenth century and the psychological perception of its author is not its only remarkable feature. What makes the novel so effective is its style, written as it is with 'the pen of Mirth and the ink of Melancholy', as Machado de Assis says of the composition of his earlier masterpiece, *Epitaph of a Small Winner*. The style is partly derived from the Laurence Sterne of *A Sentimental Journey*—very short chapters which are sometimes devoted to seemingly trivial details with a fine sense of the absurd and the comical attending his observation of reality. Machado's tone, which is entirely his own, and his melancholy mirth are very modern: one observes them, for example, in Italo Svevo.

To see something of Machado's genius, examine the narrative technique of *Dom Casmurro*.

When Bento has no recourse but to enter the seminary, Dom Casmurro reaches a point in his narrative when he must tell of those years. 'Ah! I am not going to tell the story of the seminary;' he declares, and then adds, 'Some day, yes, it is possible that I will compose a brief account of what I saw there and the life I led, of those I lived with, of the customs and all the rest.' The reader gets the hint: Machado does not want to become involved with the subject matter which is not quite relevant to his main theme and is inviting the reader to imagine what life at the seminary must have been like and leave him to proceed with the important events of the story. No sooner does the reader allow him this privilege than Machado plays a sly trick, for he makes Dom Casmurro proceed with what appears to be a greater irrelevance than a description of life at the seminary would have been: 'This itch to write, when you catch it at fifty, never leaves you. In youth it is possible for a man to cure himself of it; and, without going any further, right here in the seminary I had a comrade who composed verses.'

The comrade had gone on to take orders; when Bento runs into him at a church some years later he asks him to show him his latest verses. The priest is startled by the request. 'He confessed he had not written any verses since he was ordained. It had been a tickling of youth; he scratched, it went away, he was well.'

This episode brings another to Bento's mind. He remembers another seminarist who had composed a *Panegyric of Saint Monica* which had been so successful at the seminary that the young author had had copies printed and distributed, giving one to Bento. When Bento ran into him twenty-six years later, he found that the young man had abandoned ideas of a priesthood as well as of literature and had become a bureaucrat; but he remembered the *Panegyric* as the high point of his earlier years. After they have exchanged a few remarks about their days at the seminary, the man asks, 'Did you keep my *Panegyric*?' Bento has no idea of what he is talking about, but mumbles an excuse. The next day the man brings him a copy of the *Panegyric*, 'a little old book, twenty-six years old, soiled, mottled with age'. It is evident that the opusculum is a piece of nonsense, but Bento is polite to his former comrade and enthusiastically recalls 'those days of fellowship, the padres, the lessons, the games.' But the classmate is scarcely listening; for him the seminary evokes only one memory, the glory he won as the author of the *Panegyric*, and he leaves Bento, saying, 'People have liked it, this *Panegyric* of mine!'

The *Panegyric* reminds Bento of the time in the seminary when he himself was inspired to compose a sonnet. He lay in bed and suddenly a line came to him:

> *O flower of heaven! O flower bright and pure!*

He realizes that the words sound like a line of verse and decides to compose 'something to go with it, a sonnet.'

> The tickling asked for finger-nails. I scratched with my whole soul. I did not choose the sonnet right away. At first I considered other forms, rhymed as well as blank verse, but finally I settled on the sonnet: a poem that was brief and adaptable. As for the idea, the first verse was not yet an idea, it was an exclamation; the idea would come later. Thus, lying in bed, wrapped up in the sheet, I essayed to poeticize.

He repeats the line, finding it compellingly beautiful, and waits for the rest of the sonnet to come to him. It does not. Even after he has recited the first line while lying on his right side, then on his left and finally on his back, nothing else comes. No posture seems propitious. He decides that what he needs is not the next line but the final line of the sonnet, for the final line must be a kind of 'a golden key . . . one of those verses which are a triumph of thought and form.' After considerable effort, he comes up with:

Life is lost, the battle still is won!

The 'flower of heaven', which he had first thought to be an image of Capitú, can now, he decides, serve as an image for *justice*; but he changes his mind again: the flower should stand for *charity*—a thought more appropriate for a seminarist. Now he is all set to produce a beautiful poem: 'The feeling I had was that a perfect sonnet was about to be born.' But the middle lines refuse to come. He has 'several fits of rage' but his mind remains blank until he has a brilliant notion: what about transposing two of the words of the last line so that it reads:

Life is won, the battle still is lost!

By making this change, he perceives that the 'meaning turns out to be exactly the opposite, but perhaps this in itself would coax inspiration. In this case, it would be irony.' But inspiration will not be coaxed and the sonnet is abandoned with those two lines left in a corner like crutches with no body to support. At the end of the chapter, Machado offers the two lines to 'the first idle soul who wants them. On a Sunday, or if it's raining, or in the country, or in any other moments of leisure, he can try to see if the sonnet will come. All he has to do is to give it an idea and fill in the missing middle.'

Perhaps only other writers will appreciate the humour and satire of this chapter, 'A Sonnet'. The seemingly innocent and polite closing lines, as quoted above, which appear to confirm the common notion that writing is a hobby to be indulged on a Sunday, that it is simply a matter of finding an idea to fill up a gap, are quite ferociously satirical, for the words are being written by

Dom Casmurro who knows very well how much of his life he is giving to the composition of his book. But what has the frustrated sonnet got to do with the seminary? It has been an association which has come from seeing the *Panegyric* which, like Proust's madeleine, has evoked a host of memories. But the memories of the years at the seminary were evoked twenty-six years after the events there while Dom Casmurro is recording the evocation of the memories several years later still during which time he has married and then lost his family and friends. By creating the narrative of the seminary years from the perspective of twenty-six years later, while making the year in which the *Panegyric* is again seen itself a memory of the remote past, Machado can therefore reveal both the past and the future. It is the *Panegyric* which again shows Casmurro the face of the young Escobar, and by bringing him into the narrative and creating the years of the early friendship between him and Bento, Machado effects a neat reversal in his treatment of time: what is evoked of the past has become the present and the chronology which seemed to suffer a gap has in fact remained undisturbed.

During the years when Bento is at the seminary he returns home for weekends and for a longer period once when his mother is ill. It is on one of these occasions that we read one of the best examples in Machado of what can be called the irrelevant episode. Bento is walking down the street, his mind full of his love for Capitú when a voice calls him to a house. A boy of about his age, named Manduca, has just died of leprosy. Bento is revolted by the sight of the dead boy but is pleased to have the opportunity to honour the funeral with his presence because it gives him an excuse to delay his return to the seminary, thus creating for himself an occasion 'to pay another visit to Capitú, a more extended visit.' His wish is denied by his family and he has to return to the seminary, but the episode leads him to have a memory of the very brief relationship he had had with Manduca two years earlier.

They had exchanged a correspondence on the Crimean War! The chapter recording that correspondence is called 'The Polemic' and is one of the most beautiful and funny chapters in the novel. Manduca ends each of his letters with a passionate 'The Russians will not enter Constantinople!' while Bento, obliged to take an opposing position, disagrees. Bento has no real interest in the outcome of the Crimean War since he has at the time, as he says, 'a thousand other things to distract me—school, diversions, family, and my own robust health which called me to other exercises.' Manduca, dying of leprosy, has only the Crimean War to exercise him since it is the issue most talked about in the papers. The mind within the dying body is holding on to a staggeringly bold physical action, the defence of the Allies against Russia! His last days are made tolerable by the thought that the Russians will not enter Constantinople. The chapter is irrelevant and yet the episode it records is of the very essence of reality which is inevitably composed of such unreal situations; it is only human vanity, when it is engaged in creating a fiction of one's past self, which forgets the trivialities which surround one's reality.

There are two more of several such irrelevant episodes which are memorable in *Dom Casmurro*. The first, early in the novel, concerns an Italian tenor who believes that 'Life is an opera.' He elaborates his theory:

God is the poet. The music is by Satan, a young maestro with a great future, who studied in the conservatory of heaven. Rival of Michael, Raphael, and Gabriel, he could not endure the priority those classmates enjoyed in the distribution of the prizes. It may be, too, that their overly sweet and mystic music was boring to his genius, which was essentially tragic. He started a rebellion, which was discovered in time, and he was expelled from the conservatory. The whole thing would have ended there, if God had not written a libretto for an opera, and thrown it aside, because he considered that type of amusement unsuited to his eternity.

Satan takes the manuscript and his resentment off to hell; determined like any outcast to show himself to be superior to the respected members of the conservatory, he composes a score for the discarded libretto and takes it to God in an understandable attempt to ingratiate himself to His favour. God refuses to hear it. Like any poor composer before an impresario, Satan continues to persist; and God finally 'consented to have the opera performed, but outside the precincts of heaven.' It was for the sake of this wretched opera that God 'designed a special theatre', the planet earth, but was so thoroughly bored by the project and by the pestering Satan that He refused even to hear the rehearsals. The result, the tenor goes on, has been a catastrophe.

> That refusal was probably a mistake: from it resulted certain incongruities which a hearing would have detected and a friendly collaboration prevented. Indeed in some places the words go to the right and the music to the left. And there are those who say that this is the beauty of the composition and keeps it from being monotonous, and in this way they explain the trio of Eden, the aria of Abel, the choruses of the guillotine and slavery. Not infrequently the same plot situation is used over again without sufficient reason.

This enormous opera will continue to run until the theatre in which it is being played lasts, — 'and there's no telling when *it* will be demolished as an act of astronomic expediency.' All great dramas are taken from this opera, even Shakespeare is a plagiarist. And a novel called *Dom Casmurro* is a fragment of action in this opera where a number of people have been fated to play the ridiculous parts assigned to them for no particular reason.

The starting point of the tenor's theory appears ludicrous but by the time he finishes his little narrative he seems to have told a story which might have been written by Borges. The fiction of a planet created for rehearsing an opera which God refuses to see after allowing the stage to be set is little different from the fiction called 'Tlön, Uqbar, Orbis Tertius'. And of course it is not altogether irrelevant in *Dom Casmurro* since its idea of events being staged ties up with the theatre imagery of the novel; there is also the implication that if these characters are only a few dots in a remote corner of the theatre and their actions of no real bearing on the grand opera, then even the pain they are obliged to endure is either meaningless or a trivial little farce which the audience does not notice.

The second memorable irrelevant episode occurs towards the end of the novel, when Bento is returning from Escobar's funeral. The neighbourhood barber happens to be playing on his fiddle and noticing that he has an audience in Bento, he plays with greater ardour, losing a couple of customers in the process. A crowd begins to gather. The barber plays on, losing the money for the next day's bread but surfeited for the moment by the admiration of the audience. It is a perfect example of the way reality operates. A fiction narrating a tragedy is obliged to pause and to observe the larger human comedy of which even a tragedy has to be composed.

The copy of his parents' house which Bento has had built is not only a theatre in which he observes the drama of his life, it is also a symbol of the emptiness he has felt within himself since the awakening of his jealousy. And it is only after coming to live in this house that he acquires the name Dom Casmurro; and this Dom—high priest, emperor, Lord—is the Dom of emptiness. He watches over a meaningless world, avoiding having to look at his own despair by having affairs with nameless women and contemplating writing a history of the suburbs. He has acquired a mask in order not to be Bento; the nick-name,

given to him by a chance acquaintance, a poet whose
verses he did not listen to with the attention the poet's
vanity demanded, has conveniently taken away the
identity he no longer needs. His jealousy is another mask,
a metaphor, although he can never see it as such; he has
put together some very tenuous circumstantial evidence
to convince himself that Capitú had betrayed him; but in
rejecting her he is rejecting that which had given him life,
his great love for her. Why? Because she has given birth to
his son and the biological function of that love has been
fulfilled; and in rejecting the son he is expressing a
rejection of life. When he gives Ezekiel money with which
to pursue archaeology in the Middle East, he records, 'I'd
rather have given him leprosy.' The son's life is a reminder
that his own no longer has a purpose, and his vile wish for
the son is an expression of his rage against life which
giving him in his youth a wonderful vision of a perfect love
has then shown him that it was merely a way of using him
to propagate more life. Not seeing the cause of his despair,
he projects it as a monstrous jealousy; hating life for not
being anything more than an excuse to re-create itself, he
hates Capitú, the person who had given him most reason
to be. Her passing is recorded as an aside: while talking
about Ezekiel, he suddenly says, 'His mother—I believe I
have not yet mentioned she was dead and buried.' The
extraordinary manner of this revelation comes as a shock;
poor Capitú deserved more than this! Even José Dias was
given a more honourable departure than this. But one sees
the appropriateness of the words which are so banal and
matter of fact; Capitú is already dead in Bento's life, and
now it is the son's mother who has died, a fact which is of
little significance to the Dom of emptiness. The simple,
banal words constitute the most tragic line in the novel,
for they imply not only the complete annihilation of his
passion but also a profound contempt for life.

   Dom Casmurro is a tragedy and while Machado's vision
of reality was probably also tragic, his writing remains

gloriously comical. He knew it himself, coining that phrase—'the pen of Mirth and the ink of Melancholy' on the opening page of *Epitaph of a Small Winner*.

The latter book should properly be called *Posthumous Memoirs of Braz Cubas*; it was its American translator, William L. Grossman, who gave it the misleading title, *Epitaph of a Small Winner*, deriving it from the closing lines of the book. (Grossman's title could have been the suggestion of his American publisher, for he first published his translation in São Paulo under the title *Posthumous Memoirs of Braz Cubas*; it is the kind of silly tinkering some publisher's editors are given to in the interests of successfully marketing a product.)

The memoirs of Braz Cubas are 'posthumous' because they have been written by him after he has died—the first chapter records 'The Death of the Author'. If the reader is reminded of *Tristram Shandy*, Machado has already anticipated that in his note 'To the Reader' where he declares that he has 'adopted the free form of Sterne'; the note also takes care of the problem of the reader's disbelief in a narrative purported to have been produced by a dead man, 'written here in the world beyond'.

Braz Cubas, born to a wealthy family in Rio de Janeiro, spends his childhood being intolerably mischievous, a behaviour which his parents find perfectly charming. In his youth, he has an incurable infatuation for a woman named Marcella whose favours can only be won with expensive presents; he uses the family name to get credit from jewellers and since his insatiable lust for Marcella is matched by her insatiable lust for gold and diamonds he over extends the family credit until his father is obliged to put a stop to the extravagance by shipping him off to Portugal where he acquires a degree by applying his 'profound mediocrity' to the subjects taught at the University of Coimbra. He continues to dawdle in Europe until the imminent death of his mother compels him to return to Rio. He witnesses his mother's death:

Long was her agony, long and cruel, with a minute, cold, repetitious cruelty that filled me with pain and stupefaction. It was the first time that I had seen anyone die. I knew death chiefly by hearsay.

He had known death as an abstract idea—'the perfidious death of Caesar, the austere death of Socrates, the proud death of Cato. But this final duel between being and not being, death itself in painful, contracted, convulsive action, stripped of political and philosophical trappings, the death of a beloved person, I had never come face to face with anything like this.' He finds it 'obscure, incongruent, insane.' His shock is not that his mother has died but that he can no longer have faith in reality. 'I renounced everything; my spirit was stunned.'

He takes off for the hills, goes and lives in a house in Tijuca. By chance, his neighbour is an old friend of the family, Dona Eusebia who has a beautiful young daughter named Eugenia. He is attracted to her and although he accedes to his father's wish to return to the city to consider a career in politics and marriage to the beautiful young Virgilia, a marriage which would be helpful to political advancement, Cubas stays on a while longer in Tijuca, fascinated by Eugenia. But he discovers that she is lame and realizes that her deformity precludes any prospect of marrying her. He flirts with her, perhaps cruelly raising her hopes that she might win him, but he abandons her soon enough.

He enters into the life of the city with an ambition to succeed. Virgilia, the girl chosen for him by his father, marries Lobo Neves instead, a keener aspirant for political success than Cubas, but Virgilia and Cubas are drawn to each other and have a prolonged adulterous affair. They set up a woman named Dona Placida in a house which is really their house for it is there that Cubas and Virgilia carry on their affair. Virgilia becomes pregnant; Cubas is thrilled; but she has a miscarriage; her husband is made governor of a province in the north, and Cubas is left alone. Another young woman, Eulalia, enters his life and he contemplates marrying her. His political career is not going too brilliantly but it is proceeding somehow; he still has a future. But Eulalia dies of yellow fever at the age of nineteen.

Marcella and Eugenia, he is obliged to observe, also come to a miserable end. After being driven away from Marcella when his father had shipped him off to Europe, he had once accidentally seen her on returning to Rio: he happened to go into a jeweller's and sees a woman behind the counter with a 'yellow, pockmarked face'. He dwells upon her ugly, repulsive face and notes how illness had destroyed her beauty and brought her a premature old age. It is Marcella. Towards the end of his life, he spends a few years doing charitable work and 'visiting an over-crowded tenement to distribute gifts' he finds Eugenia. She refuses his charity. The episode is related in a dozen lines and is very moving. One sees her tragedy in the single sentence—'She accepted my hand, nodded politely, and shut herself in her cubicle.' From there he visits a hospital which his former passion, the once gorgeous Marcella had entered the day before and sees her 'expire a half hour later, ugly, thin, decrepit'.

Marcella's great beauty first ruined by illness and then annihilated by death; the beautiful Eugenia condemned to a humiliating life of poverty for no other reason than that she was born deformed; the mother dying painfully of cancer: Braz Cubas's observations point more and more to the meaninglessness of existence.

A man he had known at school, Quincas Borba, appears to him in a park; he has lost everything and is now a beggar and a thief; later in the novel, Borba comes into an inheritance and once again becomes a gentleman—in Borba we see the reverse of what happens to Marcella and Eugenia who decline from riches and genteel existence to disease, poverty and death. But the new-found wealth which affords him the leisure in which to develop a philosophy he calls Humanitism, which only Cubas seems to subscribe to, does not save Borba, for he goes insane and dies in Cubas's house.

In short, all of Cubas's experience involves being witness to the death of beauty, both physical and spiritual. He observes of Dona Placida that she seems to have been born for no other reason than to carry out her unfortunate destiny as the housekeeper of a house kept by two illicit lovers solely for the purpose of their unlawful love-making. In one illuminating passage, Cubas notes:

> Probably Dona Placida did not speak when she was born, but if she did, she might have said to the authors of her days, 'Here I am. Why did you summon me?' And the sacristan and his lady [her parents] naturally would have replied, 'We summoned you so that you would burn your fingers on pots and your eyes in sewing; so that you would eat little or nothing, rush around, become sick and then get well so that you might become sick again; sad today, desperate tomorrow, finally resigned, but always with your hands on the pot and your eyes on the sewing, until you wind up in the gutter or in a hospital. That is why we summoned you, in a moment of love.'

And that is what the novel is about. The experience of love which leads to the moment of procreation is blind to the misery of existence; it is no wonder that it is with a sense of triumph that Cubas says at the end of his memoirs: 'I had no more progeny, I transmitted to no one the legacy of our misery.' He at least did not add to the world's sum of misery. Flaubert makes a similar statement in one of his letters to Louise Colet: 'I desire my flesh to perish, and have no wish to transmit to anyone the troubles and ignominies of existence.' For Flaubert, it is a hopeful resolution, not to procreate; Braz Cubas, dead when he makes his statement, has succeeded. It was a matter of chance, of course, that Virgilia had a miscarriage and that Eulalia died before he could marry her; but then that itself was part of the experience which has created in him a disgust for life. In the end his view of life is no different from any of Beckett's characters; and it is interesting to remark that both these writers, while being profound pessimists, are great humorists. Machado's comical genius is as brilliant as his tragic vision is pitch black. *Dom Casmurro* and *Posthumous Memoirs of Braz Cubas* are very funny books even though they express a horror of existence.

Machado's humour can best be experienced in his short stories. Two collections, *The Psychiatrist and Other Stories* and *The Devil's Church and Other Stories*, exist in English translation, and it remains a mystery to me why they are not as universally known as are the short stories of Chekhov and Joyce. In some stories, Machado's style is very close to Chekhov's; in some the reader has the impression that he is reading Kafka. In fact, Machado is a complete master of the short story form, an original creator who seems to have arrived in his own way at the narrative techniques and style which were beginning to emerge in Europe.

Europe, however, continues to ignore him. Can one imagine a Flaubert or a Joyce who is not universally known? Machado de Assis belongs to their company but the fact has not yet been widely acknowledged.

You may be perfectly content with life. Somehow, you have been fortunate. All your obligations—the children graduated from respectable universities, the mortgage paid up or a small estate neatly established in a productive order—have been happily settled. Your hair is silver but you still enjoy a rich Havana with your cognac. Your investments keep you comfortable and you rent a villa on

the Mediterranean where you go in September to avoid
the chilly north. You take walks in the mild air, speak the
native language tolerably well. You find yourself become
an aesthete of exotic sensations. It is a benign, tolerant
world; your fastidious manners at the restaurant you
frequent in your impeccable linen suit are considered a
charming eccentricity.

But suddenly one evening when the sun has just set over
the beautiful bay and there is the laughter of girls from
under the trees on the promenade and there is still an
intensity of light over the ocean where the yachts appear
more brilliantly white than they did at noon, suddenly you
find yourself staring at darkness.

You understand nothing but a knowledge comes to you.
You feel nothing unfamiliar but a pain has entered your
body. You have no sensation but each of your senses is
overwhelmed by an inexplicable violence. Your hand
moves to your heart in an involuntary gesture as if that
were the source of your pain. But you feel no pain. Your
mouth opens as if you would scream but not even a gasp
leaves your throat.

What is this horror? It is only that. *Horror.*

The Count in Conrad's short story 'Il Conde' has been
living in Naples where the mild climate permits a painless
existence, returning to his native Bohemia only during the
warmest summer months. One day he is held up by a
'South Italian type of young man' in an alley who putting
a long knife to the Count's breast demands his possessions; the Count escapes but the shock of this encounter is
too great for him. Besides, wherever he turns, he sees more
and more of the same type of young man, each one
scowling at him. He feels obliged to leave Naples, and he
does so 'by the *train de luxe* of the International Sleeping
Car Company,' going no doubt to his grave.

The dark young men are not merely bored youths who
find in the elderly foreigner a convenient victim for their
amusement; and the story is not simply about the passing

of an aristocratic order and the emergence of a mindless
anarchy. Conrad so organizes his imagery that while he
appears to be telling a story about a barbarous event and
symbolically suggesting the decline of a civilization, at the
same time he charges the images with an abstract
meaning. The story seems to contain nothing but the facts
of reality; but it is much more than that. The art with
which it is composed is so exquisitely subtle that it is
hardly noticed. The story begins with a paragraph of one
beautifully balanced sentence:

> The first time we got into conversation was in the
> National Museum in Naples, in the rooms on the
> ground floor containing the famous collection of
> bronzes from Herculaneum and Pompeii: that marvel-
> lous legacy of antique art whose delicate perfection has
> been preserved for us by the catastrophic fury of a
> volcano.

They could as easily have got into conversation in a public
lavatory or a thousand other places; the writer's choice of
a national museum is not just an attempt to find a
dignified setting or one which would be acceptable to the
reader's expectations of realism (for a national museum is
a perfectly plausible place where two foreigners are likely
to meet); the choice is made by the writer's instinct, for of
all possible locations he has selected the one that contains the meaning central to his imagination in its
attempt to discover those images and facts which, while
appearing to tell a story, will finally reveal that meaning.
Since the National Museum is the place where those
objects are preserved which are most significant to the
nation's own sense of its past and which also represent a
civilization's highest achievements, therefore by choosing
it as a location for a point of departure for his story Conrad
can suggest ideas of Time, History, Civilization and Art
without needing to say anything about them. And the

reference to 'the catastrophic fury of a volcano', while again seeming to be merely a factual detail, beautifully suggests the eruption of a violent activity whose consequence is the preservation of a perfect form; it is the violence, too, of Time which is continuously erupting while all living creatures would wish it to preserve them in their ideal form; it could also be a reference to the artist who too is given to 'catastrophic fury', whose aim is to preserve something in its perfect form.

The second paragraph of the story begins with the sentence:

> He addressed me first, over the celebrated Resting Hermes which we had been looking at side by side.

Why 'Resting Hermes' and not any other object in the museum? Perhaps unconsciously (or deliberately) the writer's imagination has chosen the object most appropriate to the story. Hermes, both messenger and thief, is *resting*; his message remains unspoken for the moment and he is resting from his normal work. By the end of the story we will know that the Count's life will be stolen from him; this is the moment when he should be aware of what is to happen but the messenger is quiet.

The narrator goes on to describe the Count. He is 'fairly intelligent' and 'a perfectly unaffected gentleman', a man of culture with a sense of doing the correct thing. Just as the ancient Romans, who were 'expert in the art of living', came to 'this seaside in search of health', so has the Count. Not having to work for his living he works at the art of living. The narrator has the impression that he comes from Bohemia, but is not certain. 'At any rate, he was a good European—he spoke four languages.': a man, then, who transcends nationality, a clear hint that he is everyman. Possessing a fortune, he needs to do nothing but *to be*. Without a family and without national ties, a person whose history is the human race, he is the embodiment of existence. And what happens to him, as he himself tells in the rest of the story, is a revelation of what that existence means.

The narrator needs to go away to Taormina and it is during his absence that *the event* takes place which the Count describes to him when he returns. The Count informs him: 'You find me here very sad.' Now, if one is mugged in Naples or anywhere else for that matter, one does not become *very sad*. The Count's phrase is crucial to understanding what happens to him. His next statement is: 'The truth is that I have had a very—a very—how shall I say?—abominable adventure happen to me.' Again, the choice of the words *abominable adventure* states more than what actually happened. He tells his story.

After he had seen the narrator go off in the train to Taormina, he had returned to his hotel and after dining 'with a good appetite' and having smoked his cigar, he had taken a cab to the Villa Nazionale to hear some music. Just when leaving the hotel, he had remembered that 'he had a rather large sum of money' on him and he went into the office and left most of the money with the hotel's book-keeper. He took the cab to the seashore from where he entered the Villa on foot. As he walked, he observed that 'a brilliant swarm of stars hung above the land humming with voices, piled up with houses, glittering with lights—and over the silent flat shadows of the sea.' The sentence appears at first to be evoking atmosphere, building up a tension, but on a second reading one notices that Conrad has slipped in an image of the universe, and that the phrase 'silent flat shadows' contains a sense of menace. From this observation of the universe, the Count moves on in the gardens of the Villa which 'are not very well lit': he is walking in partial darkness but his eyes are 'fixed upon a distant luminous region extending nearly across the whole width of the Villa, as if the air had glowed there with its own cold, bluish, and dazzling light'. The phrase 'luminous region' describes both the area in the distance as well as the impression of the universe within him which he has just seen in the swarm of stars. In the next sentence, he observes: 'This magic spot . . . breathed out sweet sounds.' The magic spot underscores the idea of the luminous region; there is the expectation within the Count that he is about to witness some overwhelming beauty, that a rare chord is about to be heard. He has come to the Villa with the deliberate intention of wanting to listen to music—that construction of the human mind with its internal logic which, creating harmony, is suggestive of a very fine order; and just as one's appreciation of music is increased by a knowledge of the laws by which it is created so it is with the swarm of stars or the universe, the astronomer's laws give a sense of order to that enormous chaos. The Count is a man who prizes order very highly, as had been noticed when the narrator described his habits of dress and behaviour. And as he walks towards the magic spot, he is conscious of the order of the world around him; the air is filled with harmony.

> As he walked on, all these noises combined together into a piece of elaborate music whose harmonious phrases came persuasively through a great disorderly murmur of voices and shuffling of feet on the gravel of that open space. An enormous crowd immersed in the electric light, as if in a bath of some radiant and tenuous fluid shed upon their heads by luminous globes, drifted in its hundreds round the band. Hundreds more sat on chairs in more or less concentric circles, receiving unflinchingly the great waves of sonority that ebbed out into the darkness.

One almost gets the impression that the circles of humanity continue infinitely in the darkness around that magic spot of the bandstand, the source of the music which is giving them the illusion of order in the world. This enormous crowd is 'immersed' in the light and the

word 'luminous' which is repeated from the previous
paragraph echoes the 'brilliant swarms of stars' of the
paragraph before that: the distant heavenly prospect and
human activity on earth are seen simultaneously as a
dazzling vision. The words 'immersed' and 'tenuous fluid'
also suggest the ocean and the people are seen as a great
sea of humanity. And just as the Count had seen 'the silent
flat shadows of the sea', the sea of humanity is similarly
darkened by 'the South Italian type of young man, with a
colourless, clear complexion, red lips, jet-black little
moustache, and liquid black eyes so wonderfully effective
in leering or scowling'. It is an image of the devil himself.
The Count's sense of order begins to become threatened.
He withdraws from the crowd and going to the café he
finds himself sharing a table with that same type of young
man who sits moodily with his hat tilted forward. It is
death sharing his table. The Count strolls away but finds
the dark young man wandering alone in the crowd.
'It must have been the same young man, but there
were so many there of that type that he could not be
certain.'

The Count ascribes his desire to leave the area to 'the
feeling of confinement one experiences in a crowd,' not
realizing that his true feeling is one of persecution by the
image of the figure of death. The music which he had come
so deliberately to hear has no attraction for him now. He
walks away and enters an alley—a *dark* place, an area of
flat shadows—as if harmony and brilliant light have failed
him. He walks up and down the alley, and notices that a
person is sitting on a bench in a darkish area. 'The spot
being midway between two lamp-posts, the light was
faint.' One notices that this is a transformation of the
'magic spot' to its antithesis. The person sitting there is
the same type of dark young man. One would think that
the Count, seeing the young man, would quietly walk
away; instead he walks back towards the man for the *third*
time. Enjoying the 'balminess' of the night and hearing

the 'music softened delightfully by the distance', his sense
of the richness of life has not yet been violated.

But presently the youth springs up and holds a knife to
the Count's breast. The Count is obliged to surrender his
possessions. He refuses, however, to give his father's
signet ring, and closes his eyes, expecting the knife, which
is now 'against the pit of his stomach', to disembowel him.
As he stands there, with his eyes closed,

> Great waves of harmony went on flowing from the
> band.

And when he opens his eyes, he finds that the young man
has vanished: 'He was alone. He had heard nothing.' The
imagery, so precise in describing the hold-up, suggests
that the entire episode is the outward visual representation of something which has happened within the Count.
So calm and correct in his person, so convinced of a
cultivated order in the world, the Count has believed in a
harmonious universe; but the shadows have overtaken
him and an inner turbulence has erupted. Not given to
abstract thought, awareness of what the shadows mean
comes to him through symbols of disorder. Ironically, the
music he had come to hear is now the 'solemn braying by
all the trombones, with deliberately repeated bangs of the
big drum.' The sound has become a mockery of harmony,
and when 'Great waves of harmony' again fill the air, the
sound has to be doubly ironic to one just painfully made
aware of the meaningless disorder around him.

The imagery of the hold-up is also that of a heart attack.
When the Count first refers to the knife, he says, 'I felt a
pressure there'. He indicates 'a spot close under his
breastbone'. And when the young man vanishes, it is
almost as if he had never been there. The Count describes
how 'the sense of the horrid pressure had lingered' and a
'feeling of weakness came over him.' He *staggers* to the
garden seat, feeling 'as though he had held his breath for a

long time'. And he sat there, 'panting with the shock of the
reaction'. Just then:

> The band was executing, with immense bravura, the
> complicated finale. It ended with a tremendous crash.

No longer a harmony, but a *crash*. And a little later, we
read 'The Count lowered his head with the fear in his
heart of being everlastingly haunted by the vision of that
young man.' Not a perception, but a *vision*. There is
nothing for him to do but to leave Naples and die.

The event, he had said at the start of his story, had
made him 'very sad'. After one is held up, one does not
take to one's bed for a week as the Count does; nor does
one leave the country where one has been living, enjoying
a climate that is suitable to one's health. Had the story
been concerned with a believable reality, the Count would
have gone to the police. Instead, he has become very sad.
Significantly, too, he had not seen the dark young men
before he saw the flat shadows.

His sadness is a form of despair. Music has failed him;
harmony has been violated. National museums with their
record of life are only littered with petrified fragments of
lifeless matter and their pretence to possessing the history
of a civilization is only the mockery of Time. With his
perception that order is a temporary state at best, and
meaning only a provisional belief, the Count is without
any intellectual resource with which to make his chosen
habitat a bearable reality. The conditions for existence left
to him are intolerable. He cannot accept the situation and
would rather go where a permanent shadow will overtake
him.

Conrad wrote in a letter: 'It seems to me I have seen
nothing, see nothing, and will always see nothing. I would
swear there is only the void outside the walls of the room
where I am writing these lines.'

The mind, a melancholy proprietor of anguish, persists that there is a point of light around which the whirling words swarm in frenzied ellipses, and if the light is obscured it is so only temporarily, for all will be clear when the words cease from their random orbits and fall upon the page to form a sentence.

In Robbe-Grillet's novel *Jealousy*, there is a passage concerning mosquitoes attracted by the light of a lamp. 'There is no doubt the lamp draws mosquitoes; but it draws them toward its own light.' It seems at first to be only one of the many sets of objective description of *things* in the novel, and one wonders about the relevance of such imagery about the insects as follows:

> Their small size, their relative distance, their speed—all the greater the closer they fly to the source of light—keep the shapes of the bodies and wings from being recognized. It is not even possible to distinguish among the different species, not to mention naming them. They are merely particles in motion, describing more or less flattened ellipses in horizontal planes or at slight angles, cutting the elongated cylinder of the lamp at various levels.

In the course of the novel, the seeing eye which is the point of view of the narrative (there is no 'I' but an 'eye' which is both an involuntary witness of phenomena as varied as the number of banana trees in a plantation, a truck in a distant valley, the mark left by a centipede which has been squashed to death against a white wall, and the mosquitoes drawn by a lamp as well as a consciousness with its capacity for memory and jealousy) notes, with an obsession for detail, all the data which appear in its field of perception. It has already remembered several times the image of Franck killing the centipede, the Scutigera, and also the image of the marks left on the white wall. It is a novel in which there is no narrator but one which is a sequence of random and repetitive images as they occur in the sense perceptions of a living being, and is thus closer to reality than could be composed by an omniscient narrator. The situation is very simple: the person, the record of whose perceptions we are reading, is alone in a plantation house in a tropical country; his wife, given the name A . . ., and their neighbour, Franck, have gone to the nearby town and the rather long delay in their return seems to indicate that perhaps they are having an affair, or it could simply be that Franck's car has in fact broken down. The narrator, or the seeing eye, wanders about the house, and repeatedly finds himself looking at things, some before him in the present and some being re-enacted in his mind's eye from the past. The way the chairs are placed in the veranda and where each one of them sat; the recent dinner they had together when Franck rose from the table to kill the centipede; A . . .'s dressing-table and the objects on it: the narrator observes again to see what it is that he has looked at in order to perceive clearly a past event—even such a detail as the placing of a hand on an arm-chair—to see if he cannot arrive at a truth. At the same time, the life on the plantation goes on: a worker in the fields is singing a song, the banana trees are growing, the insects are drawn to the lamp. The images, which appear to be trivial and confusing, are in fact very precisely organized; and this 'new novel', *Jealousy*, with its original form can be seen to be closer to reality than any realistic novel. In it, fiction and the reality which the fiction is trying to reveal coincide in the language. Once one has grasped that the narrative is a sequence of images in the perception of a seeing eye, and has understood the person's anxiety that his wife and Franck have not returned, the novel becomes a perfect representation of jealousy itself: all the symptoms and effects of the emotion become a vivid experience, and by the end it is not a story one has read but had the experience of *jealousy* itself.

Two sorts of reality present themselves at any given moment: the immediate surfaces of things around one, and the objects of memory; with the latter are mixed one's emotions, thoughts and the whole complex of intellectual matter which contribute to making one's identity distinguishable from another's. The trees outside my window are only trees outside my window; they are objects which present their surfaces to my perception each time I happen to glance up: no statement about myself needs to include a statement about the trees outside my window in order to express any idea about myself. A redundancy of objects is present in anyone's reality. Robbe-Grillet's great achievement in *Jealousy* is that even the objects, which might seem to be redundant to the reality of the person wandering about the house and looking up at them, are vital in the revelation of jealousy in his mind, or are significant to the internal structure of the fiction in so far as they identify its processes.

Early in the novel, on its second page, is the first reference to the banana trees.

On all sides of the garden, as far as the borders of the plantation, stretches the green mass of the banana trees.

One is used to descriptions of houses and their surrounding gardens in the opening pages of a novel and at first reads the passage as a similar setting of the scene. The next paragraph looks closer at the trees:

On the right and the left, their proximity is too great, combined with the veranda's relative lack of elevation, to permit an observer stationed there to distinguish the arrangement of the trees; . . . In certain very recently replanted sectors—those where the reddish earth is just beginning to yield supremacy to foliage—it is easy enough to follow the regular perspective of the four intersecting lanes along which the young trunks are aligned.

Now, this reads differently from mere scene setting. We are being shown the operations of perception: first the eye sees 'the green mass', the generality of trees; a closer look reveals a pattern; 'an observer stationed there' implies that if a description is being stated the words are not being written by someone sitting at a desk but are being composed in the consciousness of a person at the very moment when he has that perception. It is a clue to the reader that the narrative is being presented through a seeing eye. At the same time, an abstract idea is suggested: the world first appears to us as a confused mass, and then we discover a 'regular perspective' in it, or we cut at the confusion and replace it with an order. But why, in a later passage, does Robbe-Grillet make his character *count* the trees? In one group, he counts 'thirty-two banana trees in the row'; in a second they are 'twenty-three trees deep'; and another row 'has no more than thirteen'. The preoccupation with counting goes on for several pages, and includes these two paragraphs:

> Without bothering with the order in which the actually visible banana trees and the cut banana trees occur, the sixth row gives the following numbers: twenty-two, twenty-one, twenty, nineteen—which represent respectively the rectangle, the true trapezoid, the trapezoid with a curved edge, and the same after subtracting the boles cut for the harvest.
>
> And for the following rows: twenty-three, twenty-one, twenty-one, twenty-one. Twenty-two, twenty-one, twenty, twenty. Twenty-three, twenty-one, twenty, nineteen, etc.

What is the function of all this obsessive counting? I have to interpolate a personal experience here. Some years ago,

I was in a house on a farm in Brazil and found myself alone in it when the rest of the family went for the day to a nearby city. The house with its wide veranda was not unlike the one in Robbe-Grillet's novel, and had mango trees growing around it. The hour came when the family was expected to return. I found that I had unconsciously begun to listen to the occasional cars that left the highway and came down the road which went past the house. The hour passed and no one returned. I found myself walking about the house and seeing the people who were not there, hearing again the conversation of the previous night when it had been decided to go to the city for the day, recalling all their plans and going over them again and again to see if one possessed the potential for causing a delay. At one stage, I found myself standing in the veranda, staring out at the mango trees and *counting* them!

The counting of the banana trees by the protagonist of *Jealousy* is an attempt to distract himself from his anxiety. The monotonous repetition of the numbers has a soothing effect. The compulsion to know precisely how many trees there are in each row is the mind's attempt to find a puzzle of sufficient complexity that it requires all the mind's concentration to arrive at the answer. Numbers also create the impression of certainty: if the person has satisfied himself that there are twenty, and no more and no fewer, trees in a row then he can convince himself that his perception is capable of possessing indubitable facts; if he can be certain about the trees when he is looking at them, then, it must follow, that he has reason to be certain when he is looking at the other objects of his reality, including those in his mind which come from his memory. Furthermore, the resolution of the numbers game must give him the conviction that the world around him is not a confusion of greenery but that he has the rational faculty with which to perceive its precise structure. In short, he is not going mad but is firmly, rationally in control of the facts of his life.

The recurring image of the squashed centipede is suggestive of several ideas. First we are shown via A . . . who during dinner is seen to be looking 'toward the bare wall where a blackish spot marks the place where a centipede was squashed . . .' and the sentence continues in a casual tone, '. . . last week, at the beginning of the month, perhaps the month before, or later'. The protagonist is not being vague about or indifferent to when the action occurred; for it is irrelevant to a consciousness that a historical date be attached to a past event, the fact being that memory is re-constituting the details of the event as a present occurrence. Besides, the event might not have occurred at all and the imagination's vivid observation of it might only be a heightened expectation that it is inevitably bound to happen. A historically certain fact which is unambiguous is less troublesome to the imagination than one which alters in some significant detail each time it recurs in the memory; the latter, containing a symbolic content which must be unravelled if the imagination is to come to terms with it, recurs precisely because it is lacking in certainty: it disturbs, confuses, terrifies and continues to obsess the imagination until it has revealed its true meaning or identified itself with unambiguous finality. It is this sort of image, with its awful symbolic weight, which can produce an extreme mental state—such as a powerful jealousy.

Some pages later, the seeing eye observes the image in closer detail:

The details of this stain have to be seen from quite close range, turning toward the pantry door, if its origin is to be distinguished. The image of the squashed centipede then appears not as a whole, but composed of fragments distinct enough to leave no doubt. Several pieces of the body or its appendages are outlined without any blurring, and remain reproduced with the fidelity of an anatomical drawing: one of the antennae, two curved mandibles, the head and the first joint, half of the second, three large legs. Then come the other parts, less precise: sections of legs and the partial form of a body convulsed into a question mark.

When the question is one of discovering the origin of a thing, the first task is to assemble all the facts which constitute the appearance of that thing. But the thing does not appear in its entirety; only fragments are to be observed, and the human intellect is obliged to deduce a reality from that partial observation. Factual observation is sometimes insufficient, and a metaphor, which is a form of a hypothesis, needs to be introduced. The stain left by the centipede looks like a question mark, and that is both a precise image as well as a reference to the protagonist's baffled state of mind.

It is only after the above two references have been made that the incident of the centipede, as happening in immediate reality, is described. The three are at dinner when A . . . notices the centipede on the wall. The seeing eye records its appearance with scientific objectivity: 'On the light-coloured paint of the partition opposite A . . . , a common Scutigera of average size . . . has appeared . . . . The creature is easy to identify thanks to the development of its legs, especially on the posterior portion.' A . . . appears to be a little terrified, and we read that she 'has not moved since her discovery'—a rather odd word in the circumstances, *discovery*, but its precise relevance will presently be noted. Significantly, A . . .'s husband, the protagonist, does nothing but continue to observe, and it is Franck who stands up, 'holding his napkin in his hand.' As he approaches the wall,

A . . . seems to be breathing a little faster, but this may be an illusion. Her left hand gradually closes over her knife.

Her response seems to be one of excessive tension since there is nothing singular about the appearance of a centipede in an old house in the tropics, as the protagonist himself has noted. The centipede, finding itself threatened, begins to descend 'while the wadded napkin falls on it, faster still'. At that moment, the seeing eye observes that A . . .'s hand 'has clenched around the knife handle'. The centipede has been killed and 'the paint is marked with a dark shape, a tiny arc twisted into a question mark, blurred on one side, in places surrounded by more tenuous signs, from which A . . . has still not taken her eyes.' The *signs* are *tenuous*; we have observed an event but we have not understood what has happened. What has been A . . .'s 'discovery' that she continues to stare at it with such amazement and which seems to have made her breathless?

A variation is introduced in the next appearance of the centipede imagery:

> Franck, who has said nothing, looks at A . . . again. Then he stands up, noiselessly. A . . . moves no more than the centipede while Franck approaches the wall, his napkin wadded up in his hand.
>
> The hand with tapering fingers has clenched into a fist on the white cloth.

A . . . is no longer clenching a knife but a white cloth, perhaps the table-cloth. In a succeeding reference, her hand is again observed to be clenching a white cloth, but that statement is followed by a description of her hand. 'On the ring finger gleams a thin ribbon of gold that barely rises above the flesh.' And it is on this hand that 'Franck's brown, muscular hand wearing a large flat ring of the same type comes to rest'.

In yet another reference, the centipede is seen to be *in its tell-tale spot*, and we learn that it is also known as 'the "spider-centipede" or "minute-centipede," so called because of a native belief as to the rapidity of the action of its bite, supposedly mortal'.

The references to the centipede gradually become transformed into a sexual imagery. At first, the seeing eye has observed only the marks left on the wall; but as his imagination has recreated the event he has either begun to witness facets of it which had earlier been obscure to him or begun to see meanings in gestures which are entirely of his own invention. We are not expected to know the truth of what actually happened but only of what is happening in the mind suffering from jealousy. When he sees Franck's hand being placed on A . . .'s and notes the two wedding-rings, in his mind adultery has been committed. What he sees when he watches A . . . looking amazed and breathless when she has made her 'discovery' is his own discovery that something is going on between his wife and Franck; it could also be that she has discovered a feeling of lust within her and is invaded by a sudden tension and the reason why the discovery takes place when the centipede is there, clearly exposed on the wall, is that it is a symbol of her own sex since the 'spider-centipede' has the appearance of the female sexual organ. Significantly, Franck does not *hit* the centipede but *falls on it, faster still*. And, also significantly, when the protagonist imagines the event for the final time, he observes of the centipede: 'Suddenly the anterior part of the body begins to move, executing a rotation'. And 'still twisting and curling up its long legs while its mandibles rapidly open and close around its mouth in a quivering reflex.' It is an imagery which could be describing sexual intercourse.

Robbe-Grillet uses the image of the centipede to suggest another idea, that of the process of writing as marks on paper. The stain on the wall shows 'only a portion of the elements' and not the entire centipede. Reality is present as a series of partial bits of information, each needing to be rearranged and enlarged, which is to say significantly altered by the mind receiving the information, or made into an elaborate fiction, before a particular reality can appear to be complete. The protagonist, wanting to remove the stain from the wall, finds that it would not 'come off if scratched'. It seems indelible and 'looks more like brown ink impregnating the surface layer of the paint.' It is no use trying to wash the wall. 'The best solution would be to use an eraser ... the typewriter eraser, for instance'. *Ink* and *eraser* create an identification between signs and words, and the wall from which the stain is painstakingly removed is identified with paper, for the imagery of rubbing off the stain from the wall is immediately followed by an image of the protagonist looking at a pale blue sheet of paper (a letter written or received by A . . .) on which an attempt has been made to erase some of the letters. And a few paragraphs later, he sees again where A . . ., turned away from where he observes her, 'is bending over the table where the invisible hands are busy with some long-drawn-out ... task: mending a stocking, polishing nails, a tiny pencil drawing, erasing a stain or a badly chosen word'. And just as the stain on the wall has created an elaborate drama in the mind of the seeing eye similarly the words on the page, for instance the ones we look at when reading *Jealousy*, generate elaborate ideas in our minds. When we close the book, we no longer look at the words; the words themselves have become erased, but the fiction which they have lodged in our minds continues to disclose an enlarging and ever more elaborate reality.

And *that* is the point of the imagery about the mosquitoes drawn by the light of the lamp. The seeing eye observes them in minute detail, with the same concentration as had been given to the counting of the banana trees. Then comes this curious paragraph about the mosquitoes:

Besides, whether it is a question of amplitude, shape, or the more or less eccentric situation, the variations are probably incessant within the swarm. To follow them it would be necessary to differentiate individuals. Since this is impossible, a certain general unity is established within which the local crises, arrivals, departures and permutations no longer enter into account.

If the language in this paragraph had been meant to convey information only about the mosquitoes, it would appear, to say the least, a little bit eccentric. As he often does in much of his work, Robbe-Grillet is here attempting to look with the greatest precision and to transform the perception into a set of sentences which contain the maximum possible exactitude. There is an enormously complex activity going on among the mosquitoes, as in a galaxy out in space, but the perceiving naked eye can only witness the nature of the perception itself and not the particularity of events which are taking place in that field of vision. A moment later, examining the circling of the insects more closely, he records:

Against the black background they form only bright points which become increasingly brilliant as they approach the light, turning black as soon as they pass in front of the lamp with the light behind them, then recovering all their brilliance whose intensity now decreases toward the tip of the orbit.

We could be watching moons rising over some planet and going into an eclipse before again reflecting the source of light. Noting that some of the insects have fallen on the table, he observes that 'they wander there, tracing uncertain paths with many detours and problematical goals.' It is almost a description of Robbe-Grillet's method of composing a novel. The insects scattered on the table could be words on a page; the lamp the writer's mind where he alone is the witness of his dazzling idea; and the insects which go in 'loops, garlands, sudden ascents and brutal falls, changes of direction, abrupt retracings' the words which continue to elude the writer.

The 'problematical goals' of the insects is not the only veiled reference in *Jealousy* to the writer's problems of composition or a hint as to his methods. There is the song the protagonist hears—'a native tune, with incomprehensible words, or even without words'. There is a paragraph which, showing its concern with the form of the song, is clearly a hint from Robbe-Grillet about the form of his own novel:

> Because of the peculiar nature of this kind of melody, it is difficult to determine if the song is interrupted for some fortuitous reason—in relation, for instance, to the manual work the singer is performing at the same time—or whether the tune has come to its natural conclusion.

The listener, or the reader, can never know what exactly is the case. A form containing inexplicable elements in it might do so because a phone call interrupted the writer and he does not remember what it was that he had been attempting five minutes earlier and so introduces a radical change in the shape of his work, or it could be that the disjointed effect is particularly desired by the writer but his purpose remains obscure to the reader. The protagonist in *Jealousy* continues his observations on the song:

> It is doubtless the same poem continuing. If the themes sometimes blur, they only recur somewhat later, all the more clearly, virtually identical. Yet these repetitions, these tiny variations, halts, regressions, can give rise to modifications—though barely perceptible—eventually moving quite far from the point of departure.

That is exactly what Robbe-Grillet does with his variations on the centipede imagery, and the paragraph, which in itself is a perfectly precise rendering of what the protagonist is hearing, thus serves a double purpose: it records a banal event from ordinary reality, creating a sense of the presence of the world around the protagonist other than the imagery of his obsessions, and at the same time makes a general statement about the making of art, a statement which is reflective of the principles on which the novel in which it occurs is constructed.

At the very end of the novel: 'Now the dark night and the deafening racket of the crickets again engulf the garden and the veranda, all around the house.' A . . . and Franck have not returned. The protagonist's long, lonely day during which he has exercised his perception with great exactitude in order to see if he can arrive at the truth about his wife's relationship with Franck has come to a close. Now he can see nothing. There is only the 'deafening racket of the crickets', like a loud choric mockery, that invades his senses. It is meaningless, of course: only a sound in the air, an event in the universe. Now only that can happen which is in fact happening; and he can never know what it is that is happening.

The cry at the end of Chekhov's *The Three Sisters*, 'If we only knew, if we only knew!' is universal. It is the continuing anguish of not knowing and the despair that one can never know which make the thought of existence an oppressive idea. Some people turn to drugs—as if hallucinations could be adequate substitutes for knowledge. Some people take up religion and accept with a perfectly straight face the occurrence of fantastic miracles and the narration of other remarkable fictions as revealed truth. Some take up politics—as if the world could be re-arranged as a Utopia in which mindless contentment prevails. Mankind pursues a thousand activities, believing itself to be immersed in some poignant reality, when each pursuit is in fact an escape from reality or a tolerable distraction from it. Only fiction, which takes something from all activities, is committed to concern itself exclusively with reality. An imagery of things is all there can be of the world. We diagram inventions with subtle metaphors. The more incongruously improbable the identification of one thing in the image of another, the more startlingly persuasive the perception; and there is the momentary conviction of knowing the reality of the thing, that it is revealed fully to the mind via the fiction of the metaphor. But the bright light shining from the core of the vision is only an original combination of words; what is so enchanting is not the idea of the thing itself but the music inherent in the fine phrase describing that thing. A delight in reality is a function of aesthetics, not of the objects in nature. The lively figures in one's imagination, where the dancer has become the form of the dance, are only figures of speech, an invasion of the properties of a language. The swarming, whirling words never cease. And though *words, once pronounced, die* their reincarnations are infinite. They return in ever-varying combinations, from this fiction or that, and sometimes invade the self, *all my great categories of being*, in a vicious repetition of a phrase . . .

my whole life a gibberish garbled six-fold

my whole life a gibberish garbled six-fold

my whole life a gibberish

my whole life

ACKNOWLEDGEMENTS

The author and publishers wish to thank the following who have kindly given permission for the use of copyright material:

Curtis Brown (Aust.) Pty Ltd and Viking Penguin Inc. for extracts from *A Fringe of Leaves* by Patrick White (US copyright © 1976 by Patrick White); John Calder (Publishers) Ltd and The Viking Press (A Richard Seaver Book) for extracts from *Triptych* by Claude Simon, translated by Helen R. Lane; John Calder (Publishers) Ltd and Grove Press Inc. for extracts from *Project for a Revolution in New York* by Alain Robbe-Grillet, translated by Richard Howard (US copyright © 1972); from *Jealousy* by Alain Robbe-Grillet, translated by Richard Howard (US copyright © 1959), and from *How It Is* by Samuel Beckett (US copyright © 1964); Eyre & Spottiswoode and Viking Penguin Inc. for extracts from *Riders in the Chariot* by Patrick White (US copyright © 1961 by Patrick White); Farrar, Straus & Giroux, Inc. for extracts from *Epitaph for a Small Winner* by Machado de Assis, translated by William L. Grossman; The Hogarth Press Ltd, the Author's Literary Estate and Harcourt Brace Jovanovich Inc. for extracts from *Between the Acts* by Virginia Woolf; University of California Press for extracts from *Dom Casmuno* by Machado de Assis, translated by Helen Caldwell; University of Texas Press for 'The One Comprehensive Vision' by Zulfikar Ghose from *Texas Studies in Literature and Language* (© 1979).